Centers for Early Learners Throughout the Year

by
Jeri A. Carroll

illustrated by Becky J. Radtke

Cover by Jeff Van Kanegan

GOOD APPLE
1204 BUCHANAN ST., BOX 299
CARTHAGE, IL 62321-0299

SIMON & SCHUSTER *A Paramount Communications Company*

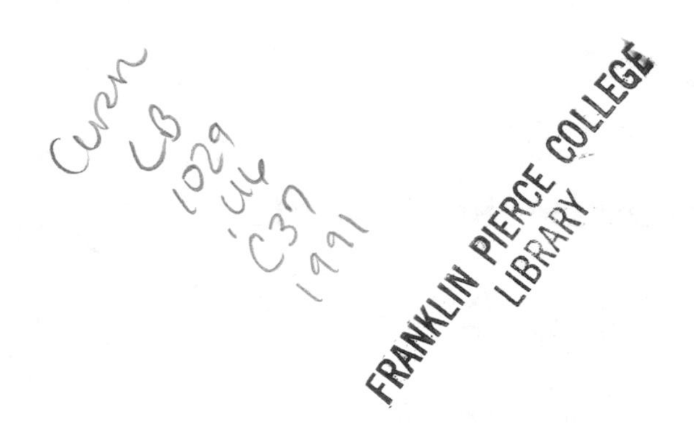

ISBN No. 0-86653-615-9

Printing No. 987654321

GOOD APPLE
1204 BUCHANAN ST., BOX 299
CARTHAGE, IL 62321-0299

Learning Centers for Early Learners

Table of Contents

Happy
Reading!

What's in This Book?

This book is designed for teachers of preschool, kindergarten, first and second grade classrooms who want to provide children with up-to-date, state-of-the-art, developmentally appropriate classrooms. Current trends, research, theory and activities have been thoroughly reviewed in order for the activities to be in compliance with the philosophies of Piaget, Montessori, NAEYC, Kamii, Gardner and others.

The author of this book taught second grade and under for fifteen years and currently trains early childhood teachers in a university setting. At the time of the writing her oldest child was in second grade and her youngest child in kindergarten. Most of the activities have been tried on her classroom children, her own children or children of her present university students.

The activities in the book are mostly geared to be presented in learning centers. However, there are also whole group activities, small group activities and independent learning activities. Other activities are provided to allow comprehensive presentation of thematic material.

The role of the teacher is that of provider of materials, equipment, time, resources and support as the children explore the meaningful materials in a natural way. The teacher spends time chatting with children, asking probing questions, observing strategies children use as they learn and evaluating the activities for use in the future.

The university student, the novice teacher, the experienced teacher, the parent, the paraprofessionals, CDA's and administrators should all be able to learn from this book. Not only are good sound ideas presented, but most often the rationale for providing them for children is given.

Part 2 of this book provides units or themes to use with the children. Remember that the majority of the time ought to be spent by the children investigating and exploring meaningful materials in a natural way. These activities are exploratory in nature and fit the areas of

- **language** (speaking, reading, writing, listening)
- **movement** (gross motor, fine motor, dance, sports, creative movement)
- **spatial relations** (eye-hand coordination, eye-foot coordination, visual motor integration, art, puzzles, mapping)
- **logico-mathematical knowledge** (math, science, classification, seriation, number, weight, size, etc.)
- **music** (song, dance, rhythm, melody, movement)
- **self** (emotions, feelings, abilities, goal setting, reality)
- **social** (helping, getting along with others, making friends, sharing, fairness, rules, giving)

Because these areas are not and should not be separated while instructing young children, they are not labeled when presented. Most activities cover one or more of the areas and are not meant to be assigned a name but are meant to be things that children will enjoy learning about. The table of contents provides a detailed outline of units and days to remember.

Most of the activities presented are given as things children can choose to do when the materials are set out on tables for children to explore. Some may need a demonstration lesson by the teacher first in order to show how to investigate or how to use the materials. Some activities should be presented to the whole group at circle time. You will have to determine which fits your teaching style best, but remember that children need to be talking and doing in order to learn.

Part 3—Standard Learning Centers—tells how to utilize Standard Centers in the classroom along with the Activity Centers suggested in Part 2. These centers are to be set up for use all year round and require very little changing or maintenance. They are the traditional centers that schools for young children have used for years. This section lists materials, space and equipment required for these centers along with center signs that can be placed in the center to label it.

Building the Child's Foundation: Developmentally Appropriate Practice for Young Children

Certainly the purpose of programs for young children has undergone changes throughout the years. Froebel's ideas that kindergarten should be like a garden for children, where they unfold while being nurtured, changed into a strongly academic program for little adults gripping pencils, laboriously and desperately trying to fit into a mold that is quite out of shape for most of them.

Presently appropriate programs for young children are those that are considered to be developmentally appropriate. Children should not fit into a mold, but programs should provide experiences where children can learn through the exploration and manipulation of meaningful objects in a way that is appropriate to each of them individually. They must be allowed to talk with each other about their findings, explorations and manipulations. Your telling them that something is, does not make it. They must find out for themselves. They are very concrete learners. They need to explore.

It is frightening to find out that some of our early childhood classrooms are more language deprived than the language deprived homes we are supposedly saving them from. If children have to sit and listen quietly, they are more likely to become interested in using carpet squares as rocking boats or tying their neighbors' shoes together than they are to listen to what you have to say.

Toss the workbooks, the work sheets and the textbooks. Try activities that help children learn. This book will provide many activities for them to enjoy.

The Teacher's Role

Just what is the role of the teacher in a developmentally appropriate classroom?

The teacher must first understand young children, what is normal for them, what is not normal for them, what they can and cannot do, what should be expected of them and what should not be expected of them, and how to handle the various learning styles of the young children without violating the teacher's own self.

The teacher must come first in the classroom in order for the children to come first. Makes no sense? In order for the children to come first in the classroom, you as the teacher must make sure that you know young children, appropriate programs for young children, the young children that you have in your classroom, your program standards, your administration.

When the children arrive, you should set the stage for them. The materials and the classroom should invite the children to explore, manipulate and investigate everything there to their hearts' desire. You set up the room and the schedule for the day or week, the structure within which they may be curious. You let them know their limits, set up routines and transitions that meet their needs. You check to make sure that things are safe and healthy so that there have to be fewer rules. The materials and the children do the teaching while you offer encouraging words, insight, questions, moral support, understanding and a good ear.

Scheduling the Day

There are many things to consider when you make out a schedule for programs for young children. You have the children, your school, your outside responsibilities and yourself to consider.

Try to Remember These Things:

Give the children as many chances as possible for active participation.

Let children work together in small groups to solve problems.

Limit the time children are sitting, being quiet and listening to you. Lecture is the most ineffective method of instruction for most young children.

Individualize the instruction as much as possible. Use the time when the children are at learning centers to do this instruction.

Vary the materials and instructional processes in the room frequently to meet the needs of the varying styles of learning.

Avoid wait time, the time children sit and wait for others to finish.

Make transitions from one subject to another or one time to another as active and meaningful as possible.

Try not to ask children to stop what they are in the middle of doing without having some respect for their desire to finish or leave to complete at another time.

Show children the schedule for each day and tell them a little about what they will be doing.

At the end of the day review the schedule for the day and ask children what they did or learned.

Be as consistent as possible with the schedule. If changes are necessary, give the children as much advanced warning as possible.

Traditional Half-Day Programs

Half-Day Preschool/Kindergarten Programs—3 Hours

8:30	Entrance Time	Children enter, are greeted and chat with their friends as they play with activities in the standard centers in the classroom. (Put "Off Limits" things away.)
8:45	Transition to Circle	Play or sing a song. Do a few finger plays as children come to circle.
8:55	Circle Time	Welcome the children. Do necessary bookwork. Talk about new materials. Outline the day's activities.
9:15	Self-Selected Learning Activities	Children have access to the standard centers in the classroom and other activities out for exploration and manipulation.
10:30	Cleanup, Bathroom and Snack	Children should clean up their areas, check to see if others need their help, go to the bathroom as it is open and pick up snacks to take with them to a table to eat. When they finish eating, they go directly to the next activity.
10:45	Gross Motor Time	Outside: Children get their coats on after snack time and the first five to eight go out with the aid to eliminate wait time. The others go outside with you. Inside: As children finish their snack, the record player can be turned on, and they do the activity until the last of them arrive at the circle. Play a couple of songs from the record(s) and sit down for instructional time.
11:05	Circle Time	Time to read a story or information about the unit and give a demonstration about how to use new materials. Involve all children.
11:15	Closing Activities	Review the day with the children.
11:25	Preparation for Leaving	Remember that coats, hats, mittens, boots and just getting in line take a long time with little children.

Half-Day Preschool/Kindergarten

Programs—2½ Hours

9:00	Entrance Time	Children enter, are greeted and chat with their friends as they play with activities in the standard centers in the classroom. (Put "Off Limits" things away.)
9:15	Circle Time	Welcome the children. Do necessary bookwork. Talk about new materials. Outline the day's activities.
9:30	Self-Selected Learning Activities	Children have access to the standard centers in the classroom and other activities out for exploration and manipulation.
10:30	Cleanup, Bathroom and Snack	Children should clean up their areas, check to see if others need their help, go to the bathroom as it is open and pick up snacks to take with them to a table to eat. When they finish eating, they go directly to the next activity.
10:45	Gross Motor Time	Outside: Children get their coats on after snack time and the first five to eight go out with the aid to eliminate wait time. The others go outside with you. Inside: As children finish their snacks, the record player can be turned on, and they can do the activity until the last of them arrives at the circle. Play a couple of songs from the record(s) and sit down for instructional time.
11:05	Circle Time	Time to read a story or information about the unit and give a demonstration about how to use new materials. Involve all children.
11:15	Closing Activities	Review the day with the children.
11:25	Preparation for Leaving	Remember that coats, hats, mittens, boots and just getting in line take a long time with little children.

Full-Day vs. Half-Day Programs

Many states and systems are going to full-day kindergarten. So far research shows that the benefits of the full-day programs outweigh the disadvantages. We must make sure, though, that we don't fall into the first grade syndrome and go back to those little adults laboriously trying to fit into the student mold.

The advantages to the full-day programs are

Children have more chances for participation and individualization.

Children have an increased opportunity to participate in special events, enrichment activities, field trips, etc.

There is more time for contact with teacher and peers.

The incidence of grade retention and special education placement may be reduced.

At-risk children may benefit from the learning environment, health screening, school lunch programs, etc.

Children with siblings at the same school can travel to and from school together.

The whole-day program decreases the cost of child care for working parents.

Transportation for the full-day program is usually provided.

More time is available for communication between parents and teachers.

Teachers have only twenty to twenty-five students daily instead of fifty to sixty.

There is more time for what we call the frills—cooking, science, music, dance, recess, gross motor activities.

More instructional time is available.

Time can be provided for rest.

Full-Day Kindergarten Programs—6 Hours

Morning

8:30	Free Play	(See half-day schedule for explanation.)
8:45	Transition to Circle Time	(See half-day schedule for explanation.)
8:55	Circle Time	(See half-day schedule for explanation.)
9:15	Self-Selected Learning Activities	(See half-day schedule for explanation.)
10:30	Rest Room/Snack/Recess	
11:00	Hard Work Time	Children are given demonstration lessons on how to cut along a line, write certain letters, and other "traditional" activities, making sure that they can be successful with these activities.

Lunch

11:30	Lunch/Recess	Make sure that children have plenty of time to eat and talk. Encourage all children to eat. Do not use food as a reward or punishment. Eat with the children if possible and enjoy yourself.

Afternoon

12:20	Free Play	(See half-day schedule for explanation.)
12:40	Rest/Circle Time	
1:00	Self-Selected Learning Activities	(See half-day schedule for explanation.)
2:00	Out-of-Room Activities (Music, PE, Library)	If you are required by your school to have someone else do these activities, request that they all be at the same time and keep the schedule as consistent each day as possible. Otherwise, do your own.

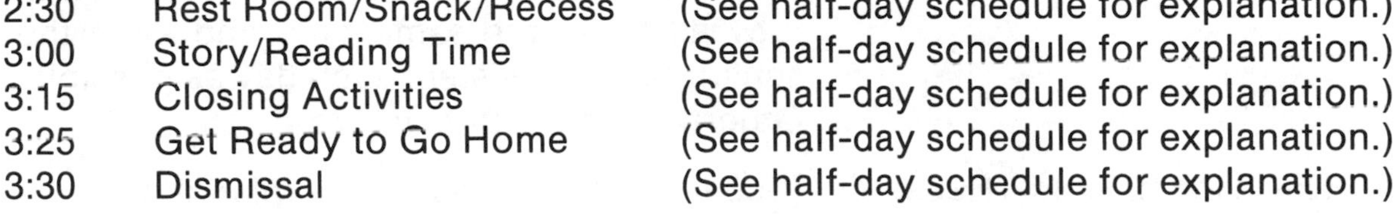

2:30	Rest Room/Snack/Recess	(See half-day schedule for explanation.)
3:00	Story/Reading Time	(See half-day schedule for explanation.)
3:15	Closing Activities	(See half-day schedule for explanation.)
3:25	Get Ready to Go Home	(See half-day schedule for explanation.)
3:30	Dismissal	(See half-day schedule for explanation.)

First or Second Grade—6 Hours

Morning		
8:30	Free Time/Get Ready	(Allow a social time to begin the day.)
8:40	Opening Exercises	(Routinely begin day with overview.)
8:50	Language Arts Block	(Combine the activities for language, spelling reading, writing and literature. When finished, activities can include integrated units of study.)
10:30	Rest Room/Snack/Recess	
10:50	Return to Language Arts Block and Integrated Unit Activities	
11:15	Math	Math instruction, guided practice and review. Other activities are available in the integrated unit.
Lunch		
12:00	Lunch/Recess	Make sure that children have plenty of time to eat and talk. Encourage all children to eat. Do not use food as a reward or punishment. Eat with the children if possible and enjoy yourself.
Afternoon		
12:40	Free Time/Socializing	Give them a few minutes to chat as they unwind from lunch and recess.
12:45	Story/SSR	Read a story to them and give them time to read to themselves.
1:00	Out-of-Room Activities (Music, PE, Library)	If you are required by your school to have someone else do these activities, request that they all be at the same time and keep the schedule as consistent each day as possible. Otherwise, do your own.
1:50	Rest Room/Snack/Recess	(See half-day schedule for explanation.)
2:10	Science/Social Studies Health Block	Integrate these subjects as much as possible using arts/crafts/music/PE.
3:15	Closing Activities	Review the day with the children.
3:25	Get Ready to Go Home	Pick up papers, get wraps, straighten up.
3:30	Dismissal	

Planning the Day
Agenda Making

Young children do best when they know what to expect. In order for them to learn the schedule of the day, post it. Because the schedule is usually subject to change, post it using the schedule strips which follow.

Each strip contains a picture clue. Post the strips in the order that things usually happen, or use clocks to indicate time. If there is a change, rearrange the schedule strips with the children present to show them that there is a change.

There are various ways to post the strips.

Laminate them. Use rubber cement to stick them to a laminated piece of poster board.
Pin to a bulletin board.
Ticky Tac them to a chalkboard.
Tape to the door.

All teachers make out their own lesson plans and know what is going to happen during the day. When the children leave the classroom the day before or when they enter the classroom first thing each day, the teachers are likely to tell the children that they are going to have a great time that day. However, it makes more sense to let the children know exactly what that great time will include.

When the children come into the classroom and all children are ready for the day, gather the children around you near a chart rack containing chart paper. After a short time of seeing what the schedule of the day is, they will know the categories and sequence of activities for each day. Ask the children to tell you what will be happening first. Rather than recording Circle Time, tell them what will be happening during circle time today. Write on the chart: "Where will the kernel land?"(See Popcorn unit.) When they tell you it is time for centers, write: "Making Popcorn Creatures."

Continue this process for the entire session. At the end of the day the child who is the leader of the day or special helper or birthday person can take the agenda home with him to "read" to his parents.

Schedule Strips

All children like to know what is in store for them each day. Our schedules cannot always be the same each day, and sometimes even we have a hard time remembering what comes next.

Try posting the schedule using schedule strips. Put them up in chronological order or with clocks to indicate time.

If the schedule has a change, change it in front of the children.

Attach the strips with Velcro, rubber cement, tacks, tape or place in a pocket chart.

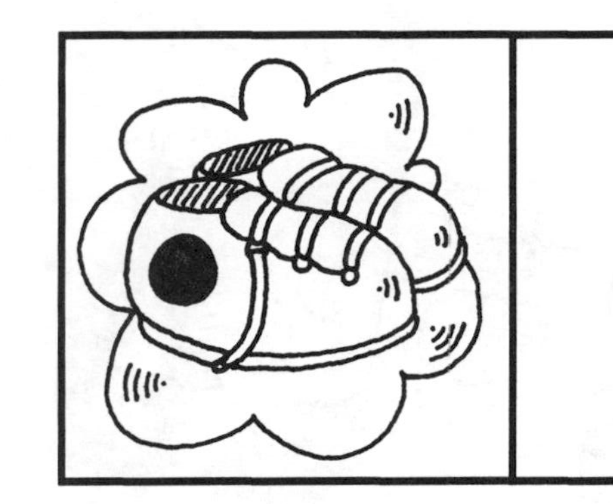

Physical Education

Art

Reading

Math

Language

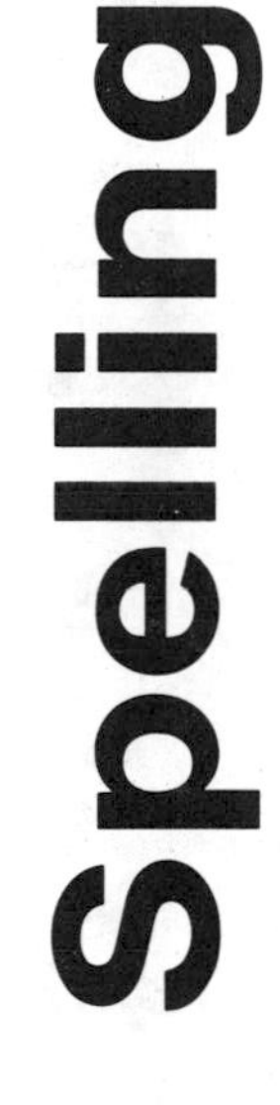

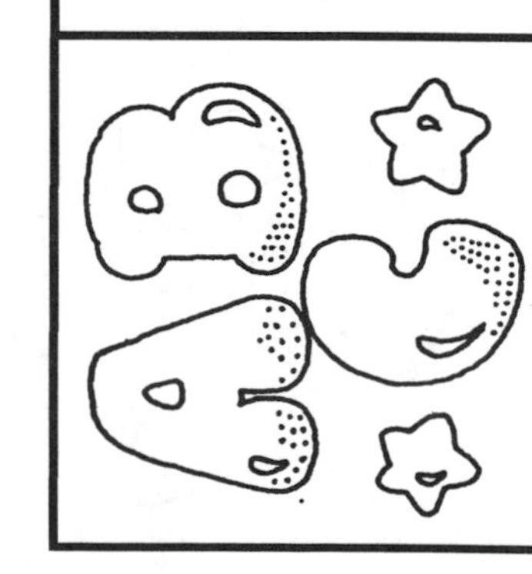

Story Time

Creative Writing

Handwriting

Free Time

Journal Writing

Silent Reading

Social Studies

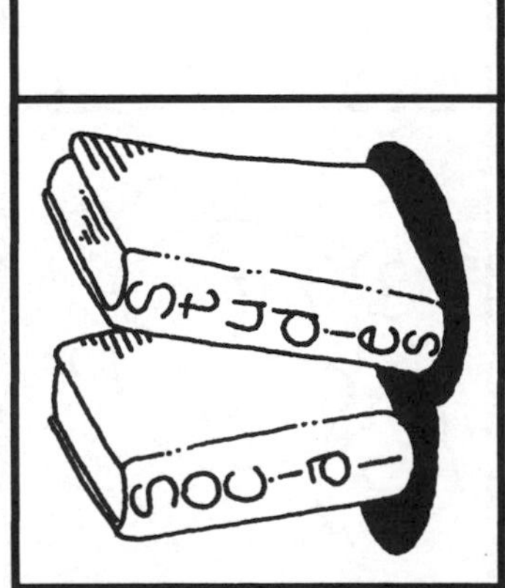

Science

History

Geography

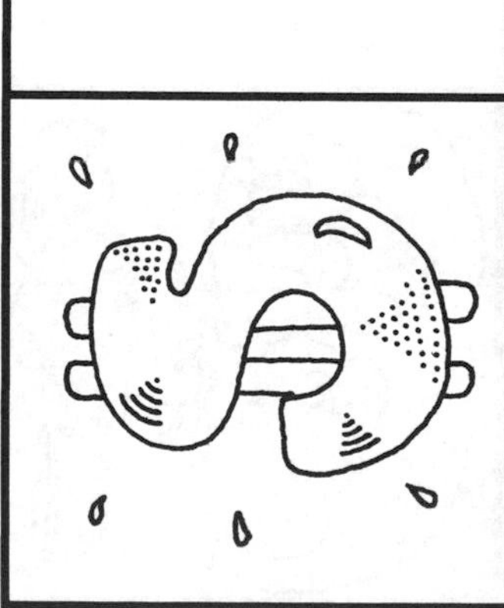

Economics

Music

A.M. Indoor Recess

A.M. Recess

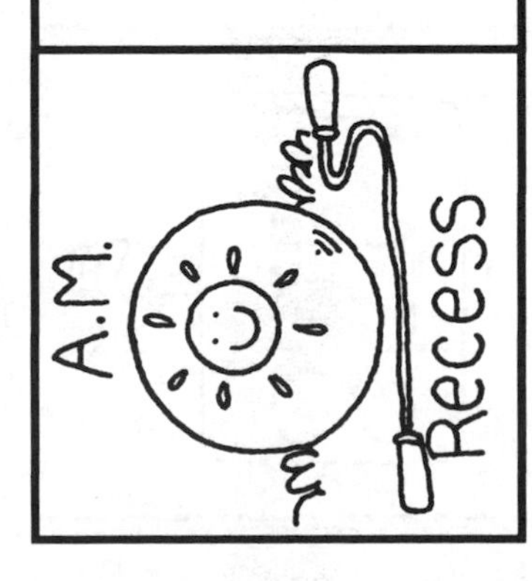

P.M. Indoor Recess

P.M. Recess

Opening

Close

Closing

SSLA Self-Selected Learning Activities

Center Time

Health

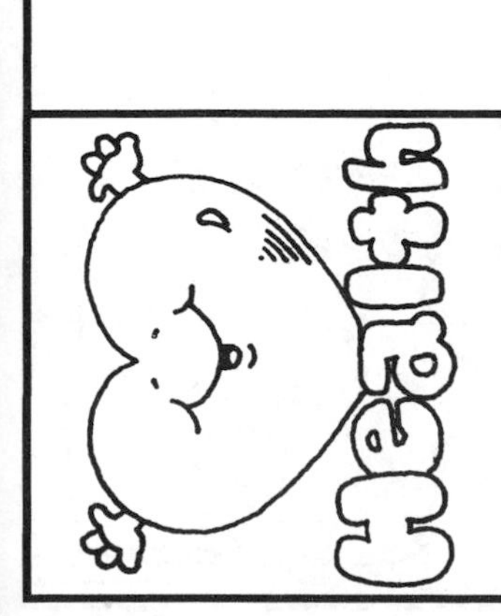

Computers

Cleanup

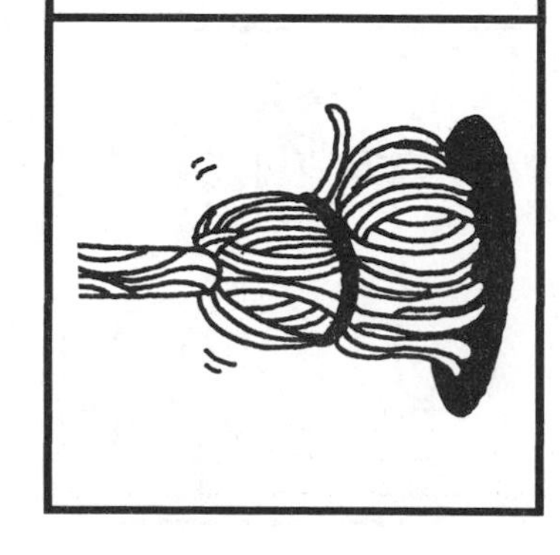

Library

Guidance

Guidance

Lunch

MILK

French

French

Spanish

Spanish

Snack

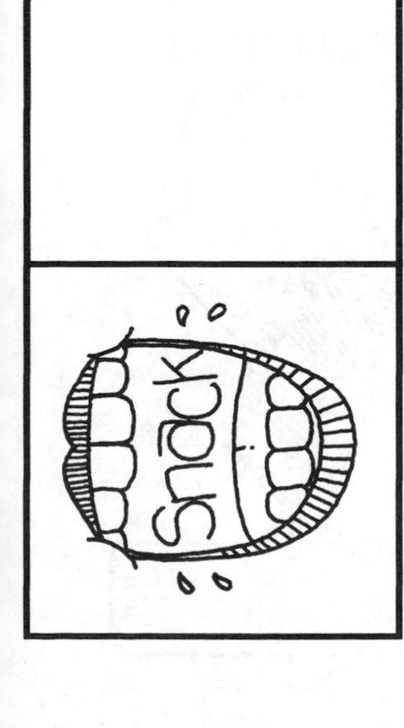

Rest Room Break

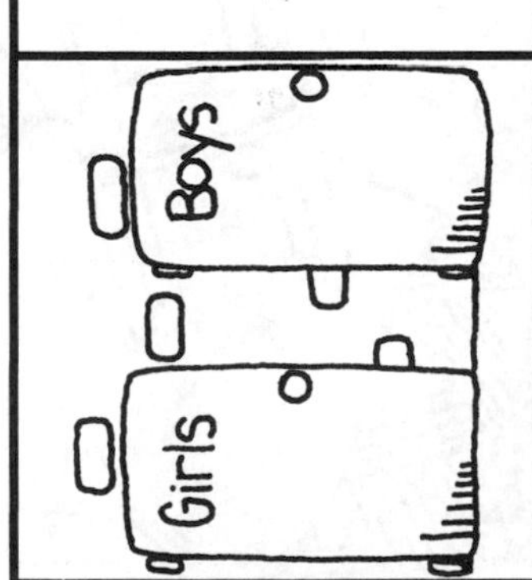

Watering

Room Arrangement

The room arrangement is a key element in the success of a program for young children. Many times we have to make do with what is given to us, and we can do that.

The room should be divided into distinct areas where children can play, work, sit, talk or be with the group. These areas should be well-outlined for the children and for the adults in the classroom.

Standard centers should be in all rooms where there are young children. These are centers where children can go when other work is finished or during a free choice/self-selected activity time. An outline of what should be in these centers follows this introduction to room arrangement. Most Standard Centers are around the edge of the room.

An area should be set aside where the children and you can sit on the floor in a circle. This area can be used for other things during center time—preferably, a gross motor area outlined by the circle on the floor. Try roller skates, jump ropes, beanbags and balls to bounce in this area.

There should be a table where the teacher can work with one or two children at a time while the others are working at their self-selected learning activities (free play). A shelf for teacher materials should be close by.

There should be a water supply in the room. In the poorest of circumstances a bucket of water in the room will suffice.

It is best to have bathrooms in the room so children can go when they have to. If young children are not allowed to go when they have to, they will go when they have to. And it is not pleasant for you, the child or the other children when this happens. If bathrooms are down the hall, request that you always have an aid to go with those who have to go.

Provide places where children can play and work together.

Provide places where children can play and work alone.

Provide a lot of time where children can talk with you on an individual basis or with other children.

Provide places where children can play and work together.

Provide places where children can play and work alone.

Provide a lot of time where children can talk with you on an individual basis or with other children.

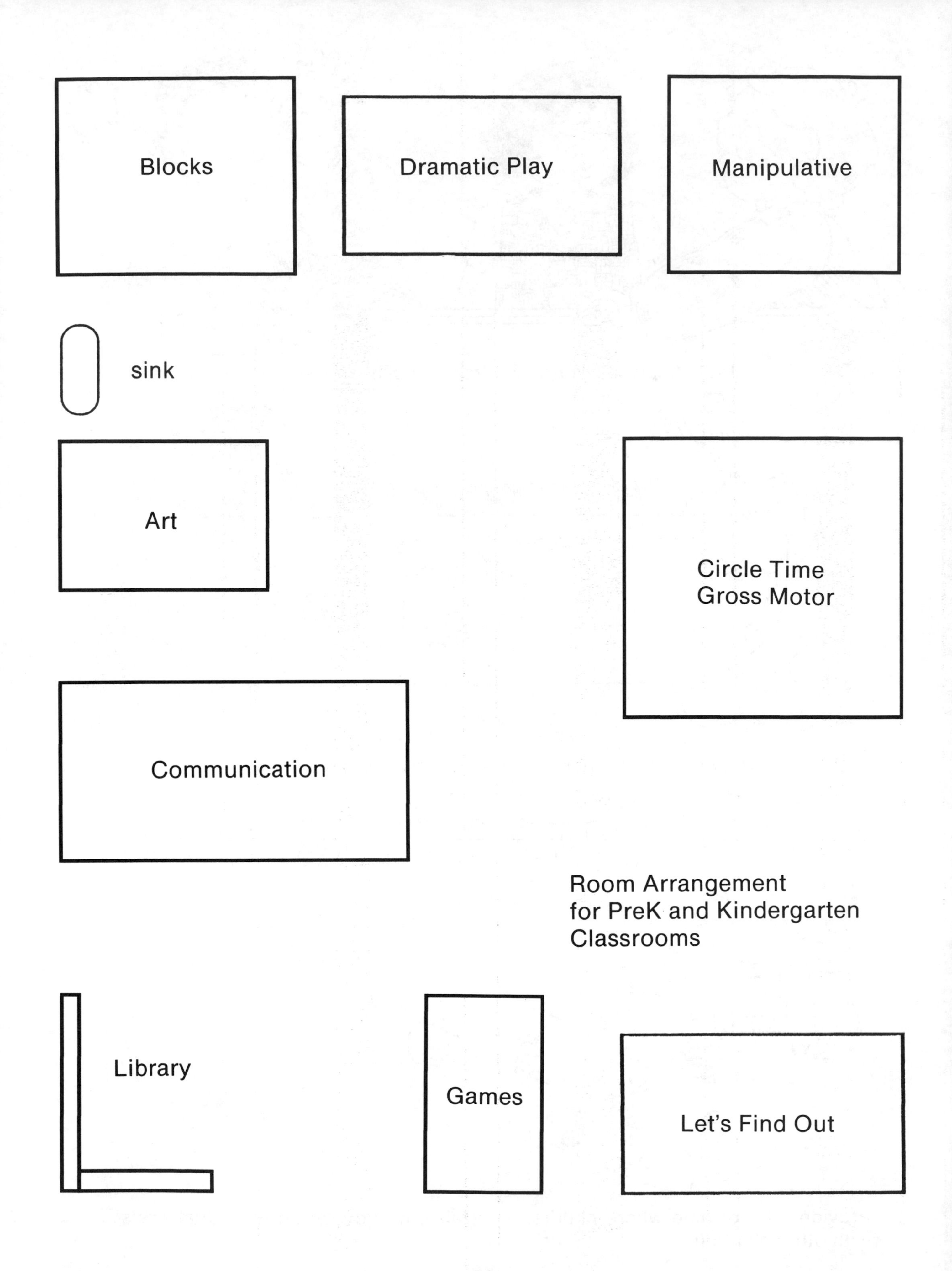
Blocks
Dramatic Play
Manipulative
sink
Art
Circle Time
Gross Motor
Communication
Room Arrangement
for PreK and Kindergarten
Classrooms
Library
Games
Let's Find Out

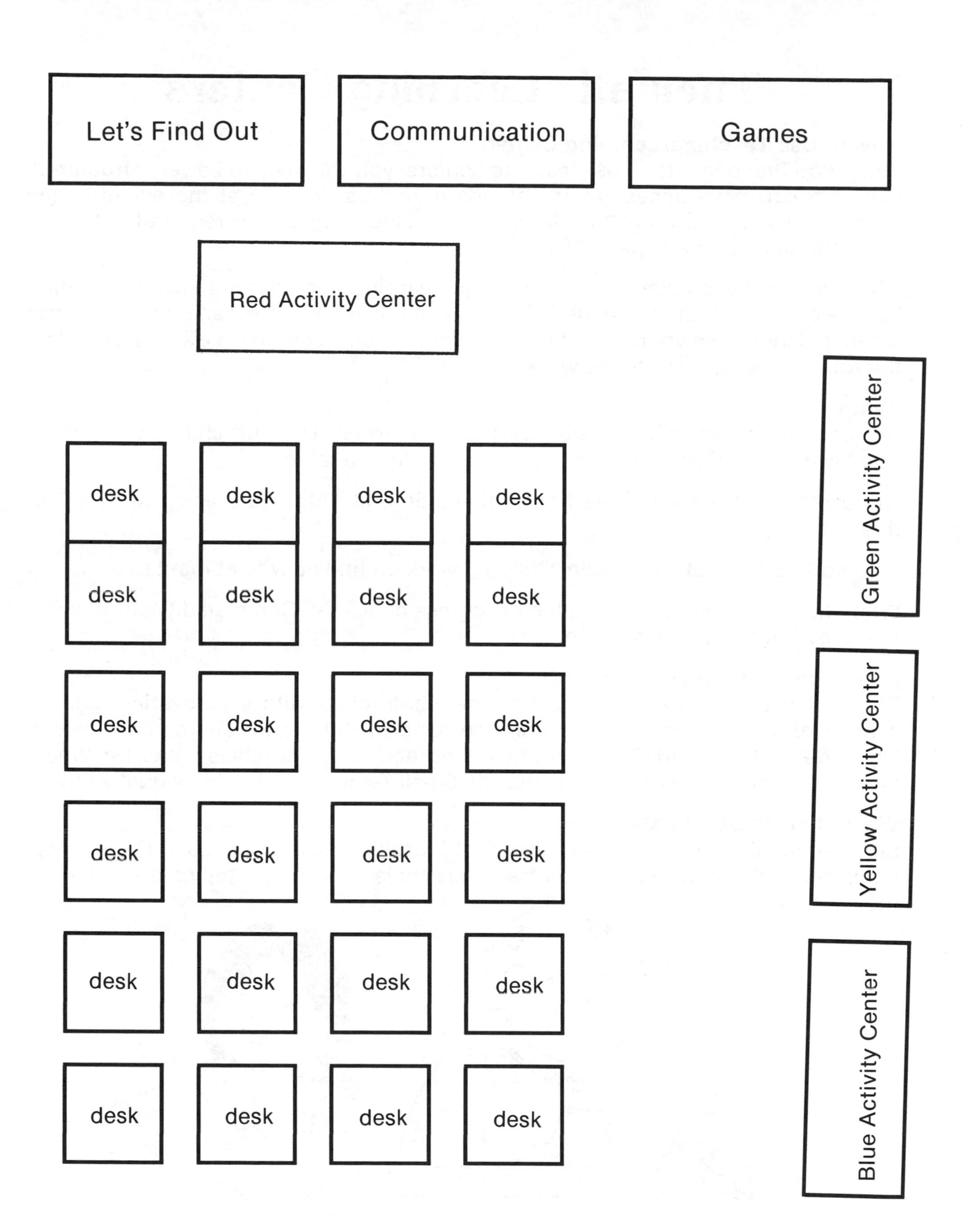

Room Arrangement for First and Second Grade Classroom

Thematic Learning Centers

How to Use Teaching/Learning Centers
When you first begin to to use learning centers, you will need to be very structured. Children can have access to the standard centers that are at the edges of the room at any time during the day or upon completion of the required activities. (See Standard Centers, page 106.)

Children can have access to the thematic learning centers on a specific rotation basis (see the schedule provided elsewhere in this book), they can go to the center when finished elsewhere, or they can work at one center a day and complete the four or five centers in one week.

Setup
Set up four tables in the center part of your room. Use the children's desks if you have desks. Combine four to six desks to form a table.

Choose four of the activities from a thematic unit. (Many are listed in Part 2 of this book.)

Place one activity at each table. Children work on that activity at that table.

When finished they can record their progress on a Task Completed Chart to show that they have accomplished the task.

Introduction of the Thematic Unit
The unit itself can be introduced to the whole class with a motivating activity, a book and a challenge to the children. One of these activities can be chosen from the units in Part 2 of this book. The activities are labeled WG for Whole Group, LC for Learning Center, SG for Small Group or I for Individual Activity.

What Themes Can Be Used
Some thematic units are provided in Part 2 of this book. *Lollipops,* a Good Apple magazine published five times a year, has units in it. Other topics are listed on the next page.

Thematic Unit Topics

Me
My School
Passover
Ladybugs
Popcorn
Pets
Grains
Touch
Taste
Animal Babies
Ocean Animals
Buttons and Bows
Structures
Dentists
Anger
Silkworms
Hanukkah
April Fools' Day
Dads
Halloween
Fact and Fantasy
Day and Night
Machines
Grandparents
Balls
Hats
Land Transportation

My Family
Winter
Machines
Kansas Day
Clouds
Jobs
Vegetables
Smell
Zoo Animals
Farm Animals
Things That Fly
Ducks and Geese
Weather
Garbage Collectors
Caring
Labor Day
Valentine
Independence Day
Moms
Indians
Gardens
Chickens
Thanksgiving
Teddy Bears
Sea
Lambs
Air Transportation

My Friends
Cats
Farms
Caterpillars
Snakes
Good and Evil
Fruits
Sight
Space Travel
Balloons
Butterflies
Potatoes
Doctors
Dishwashers
Sharing
Pilgrims
St. Patrick
Dinosaurs
Spiders
Fire Prevention
Neighborhoods
Occupations
Circus
Balloons
Snow
Twins
Water Transportation

Fall
Birds
Babies
Seeds
Worms
Summer
Meats
Hearing
Pets
Bubbles
Shoes
Socks
Nurses
Happy/Sad
Rocks
Christmas
Mice
Ducks
Tools
Monsters
Television
Beetles
Bears
Hot Air
Clothes
Pigs
Leaves

Units and Unit Boxes

When your class is organized into standard learning centers, children can be provided added activities on specific topics of interest to them. Usually these are called units, themes or courses of study.

When using a thematic approach, you must find various ways to present the information to the children in meaningful ways. They must have objects and activities that allow them to explore, manipulate and be curious about what it is they are studying. Relying on films, filmstrips, books and kits is not enough. You must have objects and activities that the children can use.

Units
Units of study are carefully organized and planned by teachers who understand young children. Each unit should have a list of goals, a list of adult resources, children's books on the topic, active activities and plenty of materials for children to explore and manipulate.

Storage of Units in Boxes
As units or themes are developed, they are easily stored in boxes of a uniform size. In each box should be the list of goals, a copy of adult resources on the topic, children's books on the topic, the materials necessary for the activities and a list of materials that are needed for the unit but are not in the box.

Storage of Unit Boxes
These boxes can then be stored on shelves, if you are lucky enough to have them.

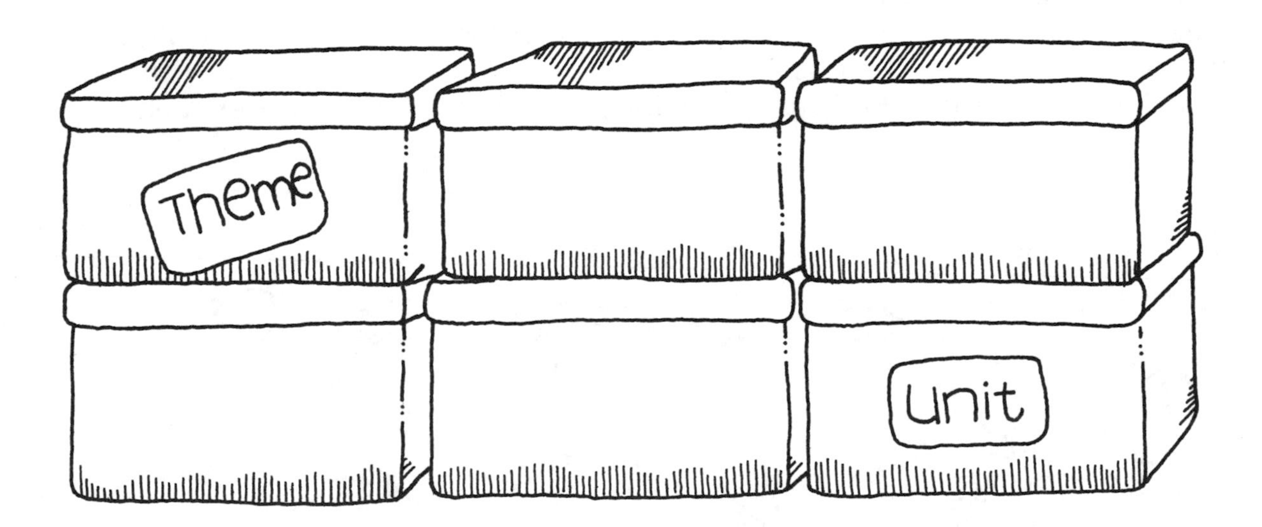

Six unit boxes stacked together make a nice table.

Use them for display areas for the children's clay objects, buildings built or pictures colored.

Room Arrangement

The standard learning centers should be around the edges of the room. The added thematic centers can be located on four tables in the center of the room.

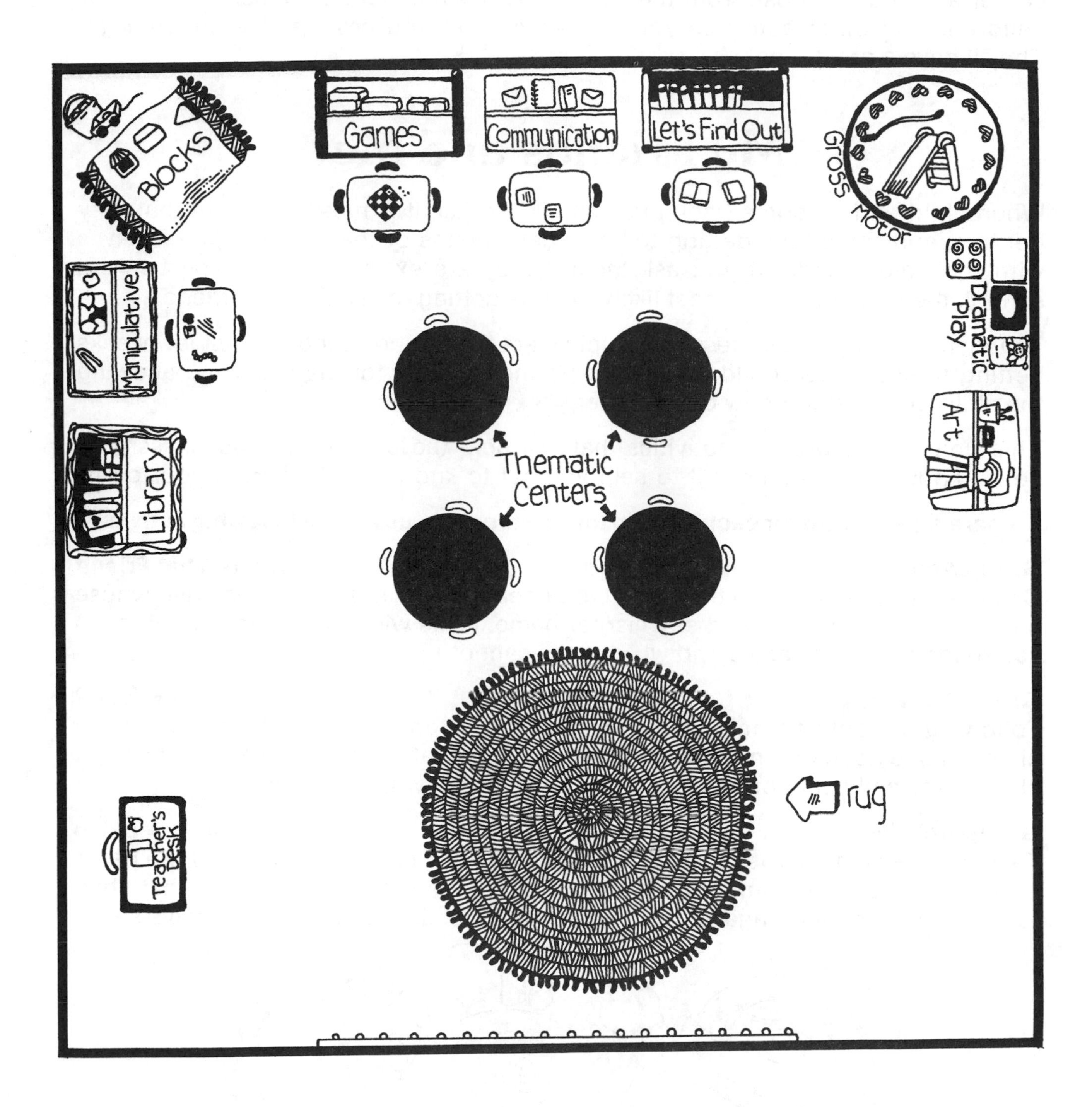

Using the Thematic Units in This Book

On the following several pages are three to four-page units of study designed specifically for young children. Each theme has an introductory paragraph about why young children might like to study this topic followed by several group or center activities. Choose from the many activities and set up the centers for your children. Add other activities you find from other sources. Let the children go! They'll have a great time.

My Friends and Me

When children first come back to school in the fall, it is most important that they get to spend some time getting to know new friends or reacquainting themselves with their old friends. If you ask them if they are excited about going back to school, their response will most likely include getting to see their old friends.

Teachers with the most effective discipline are those who spend the first few weeks getting to know their children, setting up the routines for the year, and allowing the children to get to know one another.

This unit should provide activities that will help the children in your classroom get to know one another and to help you get to know the children in your class.

Prepare a name card for each child in the classroom to use in the following activities:

Group Activity — **Name That Friend**

Call the roll by holding up the name card of each child and having the child whose name appears stand up and say his/her name. (This will also tell you which ones can recognize their names and which ones cannot.)

Group Activity — **Who's That Friend?**

Following this activity, hold up the name of a child and have a child tell you which child's name appears on the card. Have that child take the name card to the right child. If the child cannot read the name, tell him/her what the name is.

Group Activity — **Class Mix-Up**

Pass out the name cards name-side down. Ask each child to stand, read the name of the child, take the name to the child, sit in that child's seat, allowing that child to start the sequence again. Continue until all children are in the wrong seats.

Group Activity **Who Is Missing?**

When the children are pretty sure of each other's names, play Who Is Missing. Have the children sit in a circle after roll. Children hide their eyes while you go to one child, tap the child on the shoulder, and have the child go to a spot in the room where no one else can see him or her. Signal the children to open their eyes and try to see which of their friends is missing from the circle. While they are looking for their friend, sing this chant to the tune of "Are You Sleeping?"

Who is missing? Where's the friend?
Use your eyes to name the friend.

Group Activity **Will I Have a Friend?**

Read *Will I Have a Friend?* or *Timothy Goes to School* or *Morris Goes to School.*

After the story, go around the group of children and ask the question, "Will I have a friend?" Follow with the response, "Yes, my friend is ________________."
Do so until you have gone around the complete circle.

Activity Center **My New Friends at School**

Have the children make a book entitled *My New Friends at School.* Provide them with a blank book—several sheets of paper stapled together—and have them draw the pictures of the people who are in the activity center with them. If the children are able, have each child sign his or her own name on his/her page.

Activity Center **Friends Together**

Place the book *Frog and Toad Together* in the center. Read the book to the children. As they are on each page, have them discuss what the frog and toad are doing together. Other good books include:

Frog and Toad Are Friends
Frog and Toad All Year
Just for You
Just My Friend and Me

Activity Center **Getting Along**

Provide the children with several pictures of children who are fighting about things and about children who are getting along as they play. Have them sort the pictures into two piles. They will talk about these as they sort them.

Activity Center **Autograph Books**

In this center place several sheets of blank paper about 2" x 10" (5.08 x 25.4 cm). Have each child in the center sign a sheet for everyone else in the center. When the children are finished, they can go to other children in the room with a pencil and a strip of paper and collect the autographs of all the children in the room. Then they put the strips in a stack right-side up and staple the strips together. They can decorate a cover made from a strip 3" x 24" (7.62 x 60.96 cm) and cover the book to take home.

Group Activity **Friends, Hand in Hand**

Provide writing, drawing and cutting tools and paper in this center. Ask each child to draw a picture of himself/herself as tall as the piece of paper. Cut each picture out to place on the bulletin board. When placing the pictures on the bulletin board, join the children's hands.

Activity Center **Portrait of a Friend**

Put children in pairs in the center. Give each pair of children paper, crayons and a drawing mat. Have each child draw a picture of a friend and write the name of that friend at the bottom of the sheet. Frame these portraits in oval frames on the bulletin board.

Activity Center **Friendly Prints**

Dip each child's hand in thick tempera. Have children spread their fingers as they place their handprints in a circle on a large piece of paper, connecting their hands to that of the friend next to them. Label each child's hand as the child does this activity.

Activity Center **Two Hands Are Better Than One**

Work with the children in pairs.

Use two colors of tempera.

Dip each child's hand in the thick tempera of that child's choice. Let the children make prints of their hands on one side of 12" x 12" (30.48 x 30.48) construction paper. Redip the children's hands, placing one child's in one color and the other in another color. Have each child press his hand onto the friend's painted hand before making the print. Place the print on the other half of the 12" x 12" (30.48 x 30.48 cm) paper.

Group Game **Run, Friend, Run**

Group children in threes. Have each child name the others. Two children hold hands. The third gets in the circle made by their hands. Say "Run, friend, run." The friend in the center runs to find a new home. At that home, each child names the others. Change the runner two times to make sure that each child gets to be the runner. Do the game until all children have been with each other.

Grandparents' Day

Grandparents' Day is celebrated each September. In today's mobile society, many young children may not live near their grandparents and have only limited contact with people who can share their heritage and explain history and life as it was in the earlier days. Young children will enjoy talking and learning more about grandparents. Use the activities in this unit to familiarize children with grandparents and senior citizens.

Activity Center **Let's Build a Schoolhouse**

Have the children look at pictures of old schoolhouses and a picture of the building they were in as it was in earlier days. Check the school archives for this information.

Have children decorate a large stove or refrigerator box as a schoolhouse. Use paint and brushes, markers and crayons, tissue paper, construction paper, glue and tape.

Let them go inside to read books or work on chalkboard lapboards. Use the box to play Andy Over—a game children played when their grandparents were young.

Activity Center **Andy Over**

Gross motor centers are sometimes fun to set up in a classroom of young children. Use the game Andy Over as the basis for this gross motor activity. Set aside a portion of the room where children may play Andy Over by tossing the Nerf ball, beanbag or balloon over an obstacle. At home a tennis ball is great for the older children.

Activity Center **Old-time Writing**

A writing center is an important language arts area in any classroom. Equipped with lined writing paper, plain paper, pencil and crayons, it is here that the students are able to practice many language arts skills.

During a time of talk about grandparents, have the children write their words on black paper with white chalk. A brown frame can be put around the edges to make it look like a real slate. Older children can try to use a quill and ink.

Children can draw pictures or write about or to grandparents. Have them share their work during circle time or at a grandparents' celebration.

Activity Center **My Grandma Is, My Grandpa Is**

Using a large sheet of poster board marked in 1" (2.54 cm) squares, the group at the center will form a bar graph containing characteristics of their grandparents. One graph could be used for maternal grandmas, one for paternal grandpas. Use descriptors such as wears glasses, has gray hair, has a job, lives in a house, lives in an apartment, uses a cane, has false teeth. Be sure that the children generate these descriptors.

Record with a 1" (2.54 cm) square the response of each child as to whether or not their grandmas have these characteristics. To make the squares more personal, have the children put their names on the squares or the names they call their grandmas.

Activity **Marbles**

One of the games that was played in years past was marbles. Have the children place a circle on the floor either with chalk or masking tape. Several marbles are placed on the inside of the circle. Each child has a special marble called a "shooter." Staying outside the circle, the students take turns shooting their "shooters" into the circle trying to knock marbles outside of the circle.

The object of the game is to knock the most marbles out of the circle. In order to keep it noncompetitive, have a long chart that has the number of marbles in the circle on it. Each time a child knocks some out, have them color in the boxes to equal that number. When all marbles are out, the chart is full.

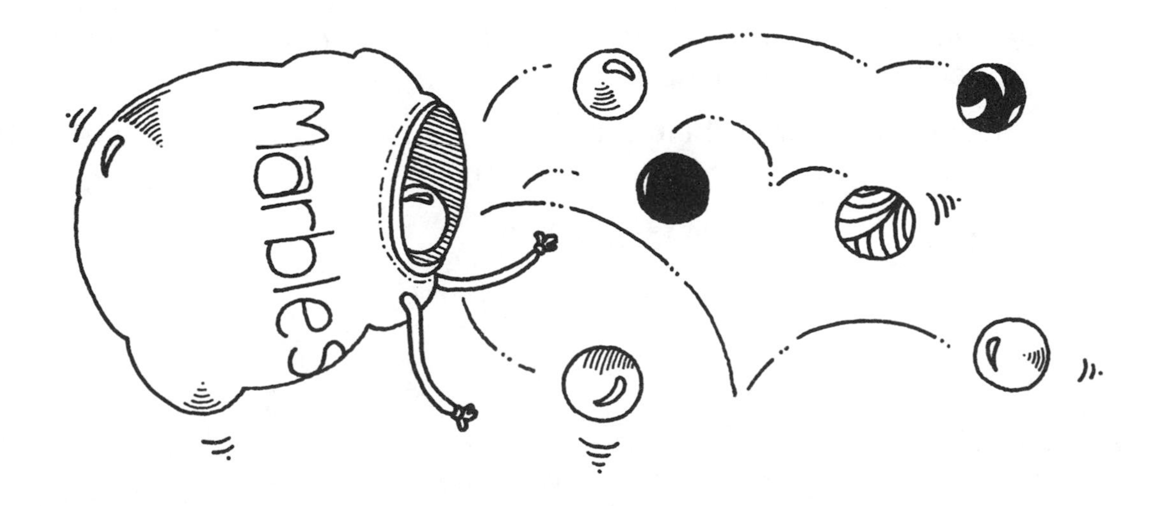

Activity Center **Grandma's Sewing Kit**

A sewing kit is always fun. Put sewing cards, thread, yarn, "needles," material swatches and buttons in a box. Let the children do with them what they can.

Activity Center **Our Quilt Story**

Make 3" (7.62 cm) squares of various kinds of material. Put these squares in a center with a piece of oaktag. Have children put the squares together in a pattern to make a quilt. *The Quilt Story* by Tomie de Paola is fun to read at this time.

Activity Center **Grandparents' Crowns**

As part of the grandparents' celebration, have the children make crowns for their grandparents.

Cut a pattern of a crown from a piece of oaktag or poster board for each child. Have available paint and brushes, stickers, glitter, aluminum foil, old jewelry stones or beads, a stapler, crayons and markers.

Let children make the crowns their way. Give it to their senior citizens at the party.

Group Activity **Aging**

Grandparents do age and they do die. Be prepared to deal with the children talking about these things. They will be quite frank. There are a couple of other de Paola books that are good for this, one about grandmothers (*Nana Upstairs, Nana Downstairs*) and one about grandfathers (*Now One Foot, Now the Other*). Both are great and can easily lead the teacher and children to tears of sadness and tears of joy.

Culminating Activity **Bring a Senior Citizen to Share**

Set aside a day when children can bring a senior citizen to school to visit and for a celebration. For those who have grandparents close, they can bring their grandparents. Have a celebration. Make the crowns suggested on the preceding page. Set up marble games on tables where the children can play with seniors. Let them play Andy Over. Take photos of the pairs, children and seniors, and put them into a quilt pattern on the bulletin board. Let some of the seniors tell about experiences when they went to school or share that information with their partners. Have the children tell their partners about what they do in school. Let the children "read" books to their friends.

Night and Day

With Halloween approaching, the study of night and day seems appropriate. Young children are usually frightened of those monsters that they see at Halloween and a study that includes some desensitization to those fears might help.

The study of night and day might include side studies about the sun, the stars, the planets, nightmares, time, routines, meals and safety.

Added materials you might need for this unit include old costumes, flashlights, measuring tools, collage materials, an old washing machine box, glow-in-the-dark paint and stars.

Group Motivating Activity **The Old Box**

Have an old washing machine box in the center of the circle for circle time activities. One end of the box should be open and a piece of black material should cover it. Let the children wonder about what they will be doing with the box.

During circle time, talk about dark. Ask children to define *dark*. (For older children, record their responses.) Wonder, "I wonder what it is like inside this box?" Ask for volunteers to go inside the box. Have children tell you about it when they get out.

In a work area, turn the box upside down and let the children paint (black) the ceiling of the box, which will be on the floor. When dry, add glow-in-the-dark stars and moon.

Place the box in an area of the room where children can play in it.

Activity Center **More Old Box Activities**

Children work in pairs. Have old costumes and masks near the box. Let one child put a costume on and enter the box. A friend enters, also. The friend shines a flashlight on the person in the costume to see what it looks like in the dark.

Activity Center **What Glows in the Dark?**

Tape several things to the inside of the box near the end of the time you will be using it. Some of them will be clothes the children wear, dark and light; fluorescent safety strips used for safety at Halloween; dark mask, light mask, etc.

Let the children enter the box, close it up tight and see what they can see. Hand them a small flashlight for a bit of light and have them name what they see.

This easily leads into a talk about Halloween safety. Provide safety strips for their use at Halloween.

Group Activity **There's a Nightmare in My Closet**

Read the story *There's a Nightmare in My Closet* to the children. Have them tell you what they think a nightmare is. Some will realize that they have bad dreams. Others will not.

Activity Center **There's a Nightmare in My Closet**

Place the junk/collage box in the art center where children can make a nightmare. Tie a piece of string to each nightmare. Display the nightmares on a black bulletin board. Hang them one at a time through a small hole in the box that the children made in the previous activity. Let children go into the box, find the nightmare, feel it and come out to describe it to a friend. See if they can remember which friend made the specific nightmare.

Group Activity **There's an Alligator Under My Bed**

Read the story *There's an Alligator Under My Bed.* Have the children tell what they have under their beds at home. Surely you will get things that are real and things that are fictitious.

Activity Center **There's an Alligator Under My Bed**

Have the children make papier-mâché alligators from long balloons and several shades of green tissue paper. Let them dry for several days and then pop the balloons. Put the completed alligators in the housekeeping area. Make a bed for the children to rest in with the alligators under their bed. The bed can be made of a baby bed mattress placed on some orange crates, the open sides of the orange crates to the outside in order that the alligators can be stored in them.

Group Activity **What Is on the Other Side of Night?**

Materials you need: dark room, flashlight, globe

Gather the children around you. Look for places they know on the globe. Place a marker on the globe and label these places. Explain that they are going to look for those places in the day and in the night/dark.

Darken the room as much as you can and gather the children around you. Shine the flashlight on one side of the globe, and have children find the things that they know on the light side of the globe. Without moving the flashlight, have the children look on the dark side of the globe for the things that they know. Conclusion: It's easier to see in the day than in the night. When one side of the globe is light, the other side is dark. When it is day on one side of the world, it is night on the other side.

Group Activity (to be put in an Activity Center) **At Work Night and Day**

Gather pictures of people at work. Laminate these. As children examine each picture, talk about what the worker does, how it might feel to do that kind of job, and whether or not most of the time the job is done during the day and/or during the night.

Try these occupations:

schoolteacher, construction worker, social worker, police officer, fireperson, doctor, nurse, production worker, mom, dad, secretary, engineer, garbage collector, cook, janitor.

At the center children can gather pictures of other workers and put them all into two categories, day workers and night workers.

Center Activity **Day and Night Pictures**

Provide children with a 6″ x 9″ (15.24 x 22.86 cm) sheet of black and a 6″ x 9″ (15.24 x 22.86 cm) sheet of white paper. Tape them down the middle. Write *Day* in black at the top of the white sheet. Write *Night* in white at the top of the black sheet. Have children draw the same picture on each side of the paper showing how it is much easier to see in the day.

Group Activity **Nursery Rhymes and Songs**

Several nursery rhymes mention night/sleeping. Have the children learn at least one of them during this study.

Wynken, Blynken, and Nod
Diddle, Diddle Dumpling
I Have a Little Shadow
Twinkle, Twinkle Little Star
Star Light, Star Bright

Songs

Sing a few of the most common lullabies for young children.

Hush, Little Baby, Don't Say a Word
All the Pretty Little Horses
Rock-a-Bye Baby
All Night, All Day

Good Books to Read

There's a Nightmare in My Closet
There's an Alligator Under My Bed
Goodnight, Moon
Sun, Moon, Stars
Bedtime for Frances
Night in the Country
What Next, Baby Bear?

Fire Prevention Week

The second week in October is usually the time to study Fire Prevention. It comes at a time close to the beginning of school which is when we study safety and at a time close to Halloween when we again need to study safety.

Critical information about young children and the study of fire is that they are very likely to try what adults demonstrate. Don't demonstrate the striking of matches. They'll try it.

Group Activity **Field Trip to the Fire Station**

Children are fascinated by fire trucks. Their noise is frightening to them. A good way to prepare them for a trip to the firehouse is to show the slides of the trip when you went last year. If you don't have slides from last year, make them from this year's group and show them to next year's group. In this way, they will know what they are looking for, what they will see, what the fire fighters might look like and the types of things the fire fighters will ask them.

Group Activity **Stop, Drop and Roll**

At large group time, have the children practice the stop, drop and roll that is necessary to keep themselves from burning if they catch on fire.

Put a record on the record player. Play the record and have the children walk around the room without bumping into their neighbors. Stop the music. When the music stops, the children stop, drop and roll, rolling until the music begins again.

Group Activity **Get Low and Go**

Follow the same procedures for the Stop, Drop and Roll activity. When the music stops, however, have the children get down on their bellies and go as fast as they can until the music starts again.

Set up an obstacle course of things that the children have to crawl under as an alternative.

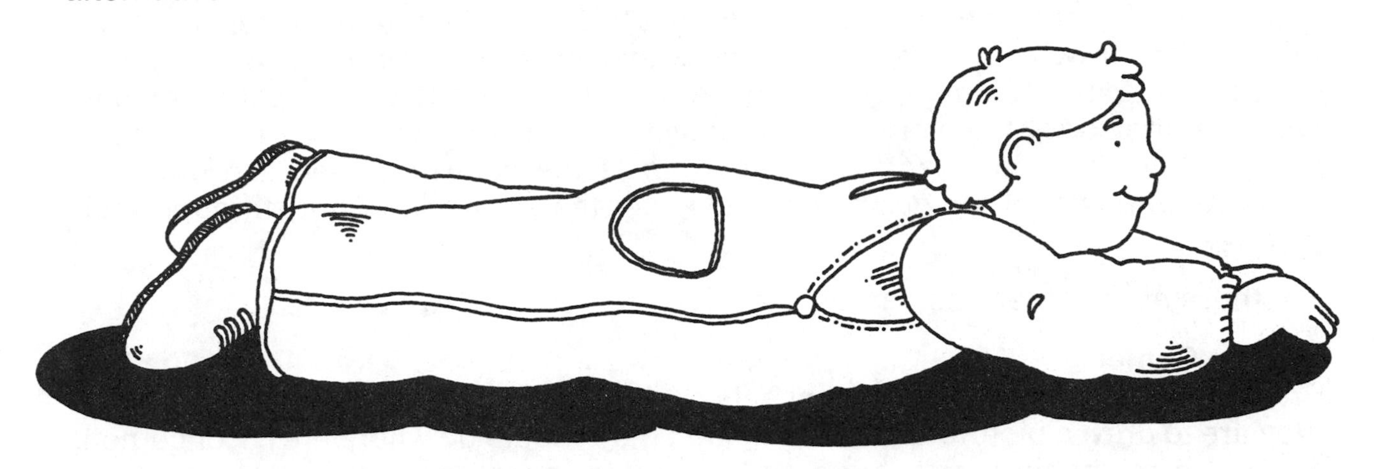

Activity Center **Easel Painting**

Provide each child with an 18" x 24" (45.72 x 60.96 cm) piece of newsprint on which to paint a fire truck. Provide them with paint the color of the fire trucks in your area. Write the name of your city on strips of paper that they can glue to their dried painting. Ladders, fire extinguishers, bells, ropes and hoses can be painted on with black later or cut out of construction paper and glued onto the dried painting.

Group Activity **Hazardous Materials**

Take the children on a walk in the school and the surrounding area looking for places that might easily attract fire—stacks of paper, stacks of rags, dead trees, grass clippings left in heaps, dry leaves, etc. When they return and are working on their "Don'ts" for their book, have them show these fire hazards as don'ts.

Activity Center **Fire Don'ts**

Provide each child with several sheets of 9" (22.86 cm) square paper. On each they are to draw a picture of something that they should not do where fire is concerned. Examples might be matches that are lit, a charcoal cooker, candles, etc. After they draw the picture, children dictate to you what they are not supposed to do. Write their comments at the bottom of the page. Children can draw the international symbol for *don't* (the circle with the slash through it) through their pictures.

Put these all together into a book and write on the cover *Fire Don'ts*.

Activity Center **Fire Dos**

Provide each child with several sheets of 9" (22.86 cm) square paper. On each they are to draw a picture of something that they should do where fire is concerned. Examples might be a telephone and 911; stop, drop and roll; get low and go; climb out the window on a ladder; touch knobs with the backs of their hands; meeting their parents in a safe meeting place; smother fires.

Put these all together into a book and write on the cover *Fire Dos*.

Popcorn

Popcorn is not only good to eat, it is also the basis for good science experiments. As children prepare corn, they can also learn about changes in form, estimate where they think popping corn will land, discover how many unpopped kernels make a cup of popped corn, etc.

Group Activity

Where Will the Kernel Land?

Sew together two large sheets and place them in the center of your circle area. Place a cutting board in the center with a popcorn popper or electric skillet on it.

Gather all the children around you asking them to make a very large circle around the outside of the sheet.

Place a few pieces of popcorn—at least one per child—in the popper and leave the lid off. Let the children chat about what you are doing and what they think will happen. Have them observe where the pieces land.

After this first exercise, give the children a piece of paper and ask them to place it where they predict the most pieces will land.

Place the maximum amount of popcorn in the popper. Sit back. Watch; observe; comment. When the popping is all done, have each child carry his/her sheet of paper with popcorn on it to the table, count the kernels and glue the popcorn to the sheet. Leave on the table to dry. Take home to help tell parents about what happened in school today.

Return the group to the edge of the sheet. Remove the hot popper. Let the children start at the edge of the sheet and eat their way to the middle.

Activity Center **Making Popcorn Creatures**

Use popped corn to make any creature or one of these below:

a snowman

a cloud

a snowstorm

Activity Center **Equal Numbers, Unequal Sizes**

On a sheet of 6" x 12" (15.24 x 30.48 cm) folded paper, have the children count out five pieces of unpopped corn and glue it to one half of the paper. On the other half, glue five pieces of popped corn. Talk about which has more (in number) and which takes up more space.

Let the children do all the numbers, 1-10 or 20.

Activity Center **Flying Corn**

As an additional flight activity, set up two large bowls near a wall. Put a sitting line about 3′ (.91 m) from the bowls. Near the starting line, place a bowl of unpopped corn (mark a *1* on the edge of it) and a bowl of popped corn (mark a *5* on it). Have the children throw the corn into the bowls and tally the number of points that they get—1 for each unpopped kernel and 5 for each popped. Listen to the comments and ask why they think it happens the way it does. Try to help them find answers to their questions.

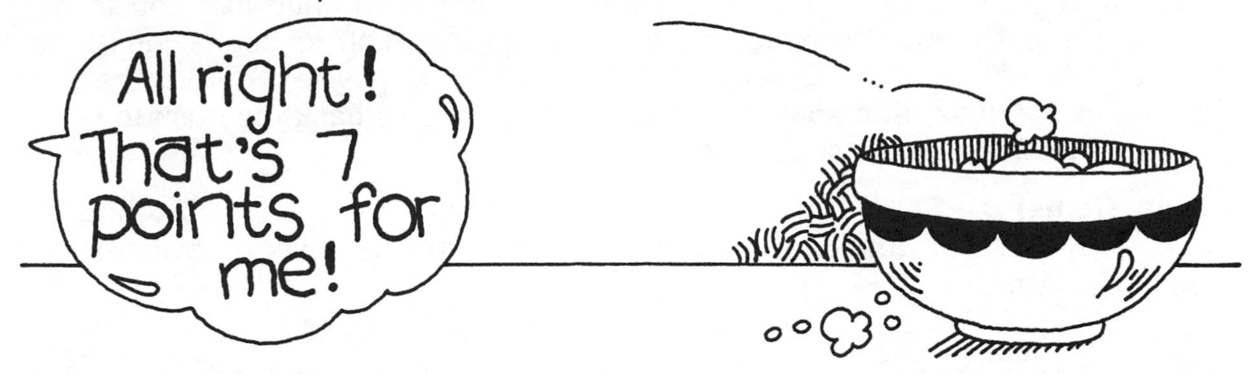

Group Activity **Wet Corn**

Set up an observation area where you place one cup (240 ml) of corn in each jar.

Jar 1	Jar 2	Jar 3
Leave lid off.	Put lid on.	Add ½ tsp. (2.5 ml) water Put lid on.

Record what the children see each day for a week.

After one week, pop half of each jar separately and see what happens.

Record what the children see and place their responses behind each jar.

After a second week, pop half of what is left in each jar.

Record what the children see and place their responses behind each jar.

Activity Center **Popcorn Balls**

Provide a recipe chart in the center to show children how to make popcorn balls—one cup (240 ml) of popped corn per child and enough warmed marshmallow creme to make it all stick together. Pour the marshmallow creme over the popped corn. Mix with a spoon. When cool enough, shape into a ball. Leave to cool. Eat.

Activity Center **Husking Corn**

Many children will not have seen corn fresh from the stalk. Bring in some and demonstrate how to husk the corn. Make sure that each child has one to husk. Provide a sheet under the area and a trash can in which to husk. Pulling each piece of silk off the corn is a great fine motor task. If you would rather cook the corn in the husk, first soak the corn in the husk, peel back the husk to remove the silks, pull the husk back up, and roast.

Activity Center **Sorting Corn**

Place many sizes of uncooked corn in one bowl. Provide several bowls in which to sort the corn.

Thanksgiving

Thanksgiving is a holiday celebrated in the United States on the third Thursday of the month of November. It is like many holidays celebrated throughout the world as a day of thanks for the harvest. In the United States we tie this celebration to the thanks given by the Colonists after their first year in the new land. It has been a national holiday since 1863 when President Lincoln declared it a national day of thanksgiving and prayer, hoping that the nation might be able to stop the Civil War through prayer. For further ideas, see the Thanksgiving section of the book *Learning About Fall & Winter Holidays,* Good Apple, Inc., 1988. This time of year is a good time to talk with children about the past and present.

Good Books to Read
Take a trip to the library to choose some good books for the unit.

If You Had Lived in Colonial Times, Ann McGovern
Sarah Morton's Day: A Day in the Life of a Pilgrim Girl
If You Had Been a Sioux Indian, Scholastic Books
The Legend of the Blue Bonnet, Tomie de Paola
The Legend of the Indian Paintbrush, Tomie de Paola
Little Chief
Red Fox and His Canoe
The Girl Who Loved Wild Horses
New True Books: *Indians, Cherokee, Apache, Maya, The Inca, Seminole, Sioux*

Group Activity **Field Trips**
Take a trip to a farm with a horse and buggy for a ride over the fields. Try a trip to a pumpkin farm. Visit local historical museums to see paraphernalia used in the olden days.

Activity Center **Bulletin Board: What's Old? What's New?**

Gather pictures of objects that show the old and the new things. A lantern, a lamp; a horse and buggy, a car; a bowl and spoon, a mixer; a mortar and pestle, a blender; a horse and plow, a tractor; a canoe, a submarine. Use the pictures for a bulletin board. Let the children sort the pictures into old and new categories, sort into matching pairs of old/new, and then post them on the bulletin board. On one side of the bulletin board put *What's Old*? On the other half put *What's New*?

Activity Center **Coloring the Natural Way**

Use natural dyes with the children. Give each a piece of muslin the shape of a bookmark. Use natural juices of blueberries, strawberries, boysenberries, pumpkin to dye the muslin. Soak in vinegar to set colors.

Soak flowers in alcohol to make natural dyes. Give each child a piece of muslin 6" x 36" (15.24 x 91.44 cm) to make a headband/belt/scarf. For more activities, see the book *The Complete Color Book,* Good Apple, 1991.

Group Activity **What a Meal!**

It is suggested that children who lived in the colonial times used no utensils and had to stand silently to eat. Let the children try this for one meal or for a snack. It is tiring and exhausting. (Author's note: After I tried this I found food stashed in cubbies/desks. The children wanted to finish as quickly as possible!)

Activity Center **Totem Poles**

Have the children bring Pringles cans from home to build a totem. Give each child a piece of 9" x 12" (22.86 x 30.48 cm) white paper. (It won't quite fit the height of the can, but just about.) Have them draw thick black lines, both straight and jagged on the paper with black tempera or blackened Elmer's glue. Let that dry for a day or two. Spray with hair spray (lacquer).

Fill in the spaces between the lines with bright paint or markers. Glue around the Pringles cans.

Activity Center **Bowling**

Children can use the Pringles cans for bowling with a small 6" (15.24 cm) rubber ball.

On the bottom of the can put a piece of paper with a number from 1 to 10 on it. Have the children fill the cans with the right number of beads. When they set up the filled cans in the shape needed for bowling, have a piece of paper with the right number on the right space. The children then place the right can on the right space.

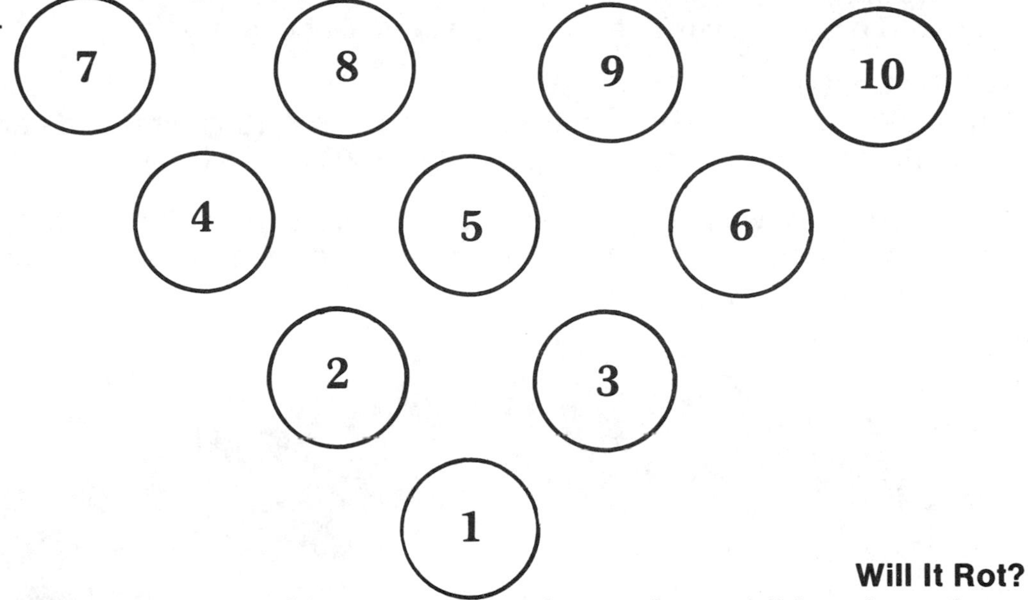

Group Activity **Will It Rot?**

In the olden times they had no refrigerators. In order to show children how these people kept their food fresh, show them dried fruits and dried meats. Place a bit of dried and fresh food out and allow to stand for a few days. Will it rot?

Group Activity **Fry Bread**

Work with the children to make the dough. Fry it in an electric frying pan away from the children. Eat plain or sprinkle with cinnamon sugar for a special treat.

3 c. (720 ml) flour
1 tsp. (5 ml) salt
4 tsp. (20 ml) baking powder
Sour milk (1 tsp. [5 ml] vinegar to 1 cup [240 ml] of milk) to make a soft dough.

Roll onto a floured surface. Cut into strips. Deep fat fry.

Activity Center **Indian Headband**

Put out several strips of construction paper 1½" (3.79 cm) wide and 6" 15.24 cm) long and at least one piece of paper 24" (60.96 cm) long and 4" (10.16 cm) wide.

Demonstrate how to fray the edges with scissors. Take the long strip and glue the feathers to one edge of the paper. Fold the paper in half to make it 2" (5.08 cm) wide. Staple the length to fit the head.

Group Activity **Celebration**

Celebrate Thanksgiving with the children and all support people in the building by cooking a shared stew. Each child brings something for the stew—you provide the meat. Children can decorate place mats, set the tables, seat the guests, serve their guests and socialize with them as they eat, thanking them for helping throughout the year.

Boots and Mittens

November and December are good times to study boots and mittens. Even if your area of the country does not have winter, there is evidence on television and in the newspapers that other places do. And if you choose not to discuss those areas of the country, Santa has boots, hangs stockings and wears large mittens. In other parts of the country the cooler weather allows some designer boots, protective boots and workmen's boots.

Take a trip to the library to stock up on some good books for the unit. Try *Boots, Shoes, Boot Weather, 3 Little Kittens, The Red Mitten, The Mitten, The Growing Up Feet, Alligator Shoes, The Mystery of the Missing Red Mitten, Tracks in the Snow, The Red Boots.*

Read the books, look for boots and mittens.

Group Activity **Don't Fall**

Set up an obstacle course for the children using large tires, taped skinny paths on the floor, blocks to step over and a table to crawl under. Place an oversized pair of boots on the child's feet and have him/her follow the arrows through the obstacle course.

Activity Center **What's That You're Making?**

Set several different sizes of boots on the floor near a long sheet of butcher paper. Put shallow layers of different colors of paints for the season in 9" x 13" (22.86 x 33.02 cm) cake pans nearby. Under close supervision, have the children make boot prints on the white butcher paper. Those who are daring can let the children wear the boots. Those not daring can have the children put the boots on their hands/arms and dip.

Group Activity **Boot! Boot! Where's the Boot?**

Children will bring their boots to school for the culminating activity, a boot parade. When they do, have a boot hunt. Make sure that the boots are marked with names. When the children are out of the room, have an aid or parent hide the boots in the room where the children can find them relatively easily. When the children enter the room, have them hunt for the boots. When they find a boot, have them take it to the child to whom it belongs. You will be surprised at how well they are able to do that.

Activity Center **Boot Hunt**

Have children go through catalogs and find boots to cut out. Place on a boot graph showing various kinds of boots.

Activity Center **My Own Mittens**

Send a mitten note home to the parents. Ask them to send one pair of mittens to school with the children.

Give each child a piece of drawing paper so that when it is folded in half, one mitten will fit on each half. Have the children trace around one of the mittens on one half of the paper. Give them some crayons and have them draw the designs from their mittens onto drawn mittens on the folded half paper, pressing hard with their crayons. Fold the paper over, rub hard on the outside of the paper with a ruler to get a print. Open up the paper and complete the second mitten.

Activity Center **A New Pair of Mittens**

Have parents send old mittens to which there is only one left. Place the mittens in a center. Have the children make paper ones to match. When they are all complete, place them in a center and let children find the matches.

Activity Center **Mittens Come in Pairs**

Give each child a precut pair of mittens or if they are old enough, have them cut out a matching pair. Provide them with bright markers. Place the children in pairs, each child with a pair of mittens. One child begins to color one of his mittens the way he wants it. The other child colors the mate to that mitten the same way. The children then color the other child's pair of mittens. These may be placed in a center where children match pairs of boots and mittens.

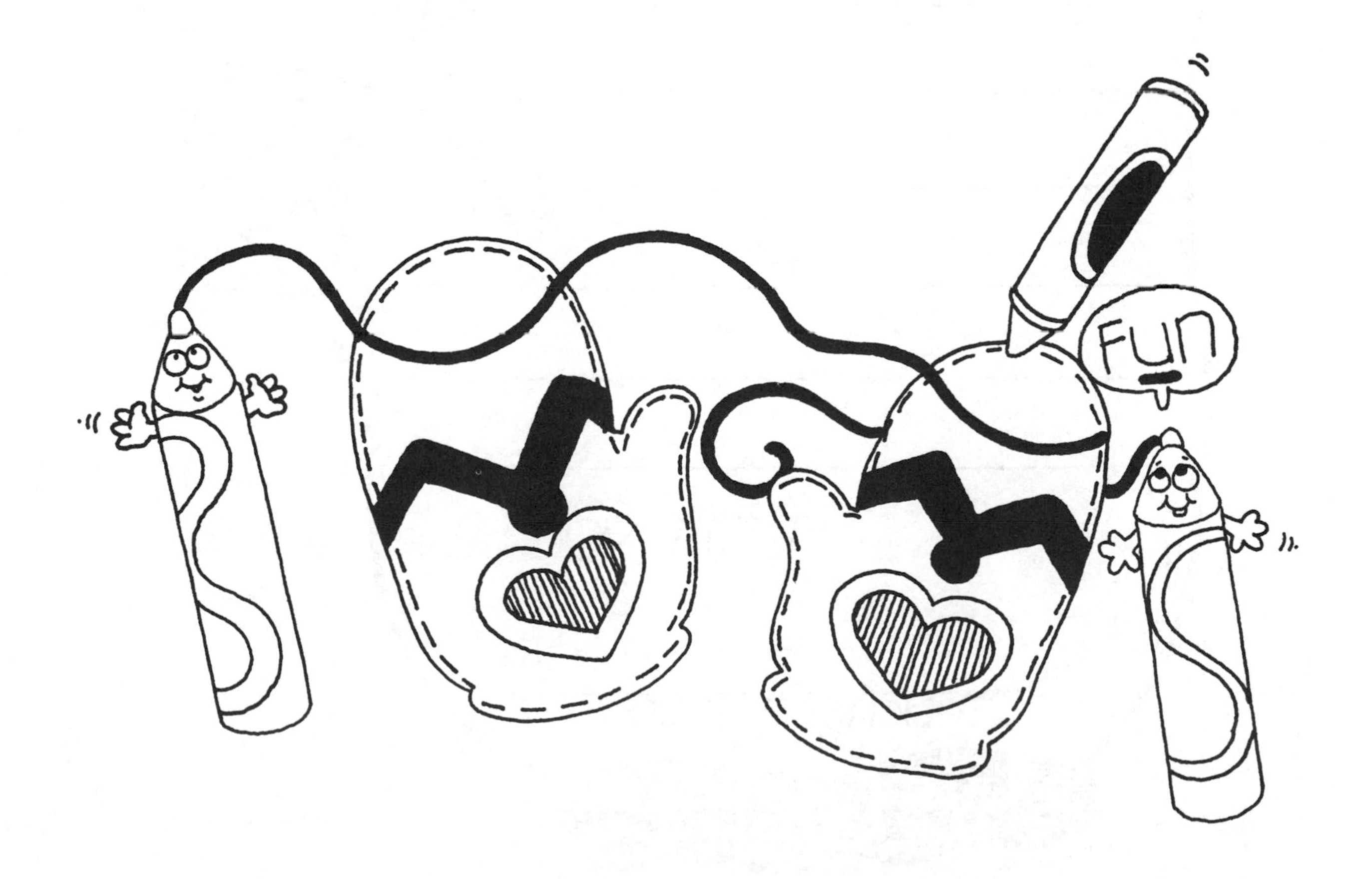

Activity Center **Gifts to Give**

Precut large boot or mitten shapes from felt of bright colors, two for each child. Have the children go around the edge with a pencil and place a dot at each finger's width around the edge as a guide where they will stitch. Give them plastic needles with yarn and have them whipstitch around the edges of their mittens or boots. Once they are finished, fill them with wrapped candy and let them take them home as a Gift to Give.

Culminating Activity **Boot Parade**

Send a boot or mitten note home to the parents and have them send children's boots or mittens to school for the parade.

Christmas

Although many schools will not allow the celebration of Christmas, it is impossible not to see that it is happening. If you use the Boots and Mittens unit just preceding this one, start this unit with the Mitten Tree group activity. Children can learn about giving, which is in the spirit of Christmas. Each of the activities that is listed can be used as Christmas activities or modified to use as non-Christmas activities.

Group Activity **Mitten Tree**

Buy an artificial tree, get a real Christmas tree, or put a tree on the bulletin board. Send home a note to parents requesting that they send a pair of mittens that the children can place on the Mitten Tree and later give to the homeless or poor in your area.

Activity Center **With Visions of Sugar Plums**

At the center have the children draw pictures of what they would like for Christmas on a cloud-shaped piece of paper. Place the finished pictures on the bulletin board entitled "With Visions of Sugar Plums." On this bulletin board should be the faces of children with their eyes shut, a quilt pulled up to their necks, and the visions posted above their heads. (Although this fits with the poem, "'Twas the Night Before Christmas," you can do it without reading the poem and have the children draw pictures of all different kinds of candy on the clouds.)

Activity Center **The Sleeping Quilt**

For the above bulletin board, have the children design the Christmas Quilt that covers the children. Give each child a 6" x 6" (15.24 x 15.24 cm) piece of white drawing paper and limit the colors in the center to two or three Christmas colors. Use red and green, blue and white, yellow and white, etc. When the pieces are all finished, place them together to make the quilt for the bulletin board.

Activity Center **How Many Days Til'?**

In this center place one precut Christmas tree of 9" x 12" (22.86 x 30.48 cm) green felt to use as a pattern. Give each child twenty-five sticky Velcro circles and have them place those sticky circles on the tree for decoration. Each child will need to make twenty-five small "ornaments" for his/her tree and place sticky Velcro on the back of each ornament. Try using miniature ornaments you can get at the hobby store; cut out felt ornaments in the shapes of stars or balls, bells, material flowers, etc.

Activity Center **Sponge-Painted Wrapping Paper**

If you plan to make a gift to send home during the season, have the children sponge-paint the wrapping paper. Give each child a piece of standard white tissue paper; a sponge in the shape of a star, tree or bell; yellow, green or red paint; and let them randomly dab paint on the paper to make wrapping paper.

Activity Center **Patterned Paper**

An alternative to the above paper is to give the children a piece of 12" x 18" (30.48 x 45.72 cm) paper, have them fold the paper six times and open it back up. That will give them several boxes to fill in. Let them choose two different seasonal things to draw. One goes in the first box, the other goes in the next. Continue in order to cover all the boxes on the paper.

Group Activity **The Twelve Days of Christmas**

Have the children learn the song of "The Twelve Days of Christmas." It is not an easy song because of all the verses. Before you have them learn it to sing for other classes, have them make the signs in the Activity Center noted below.

Line the children up in two lines, have them face each other and take six steps backwards to form the two lines necessary to sing this song. In each line there should be twelve people. Each person gets a sign and holds the sign turned toward himself until the beginning of the song.

As the children begin to sing, the people with the #1 signs turn them around. After that verse is finished, the people with the #2 signs turn them around. They continue until the last verse.

As they sing the last verse, have them turn their pictures back towards themselves.

Activity Center **The Twelve Days of Christmas**

Place twelve 12" (30.48 cm) square pieces of oaktag in this center. At the top of each piece, write one large, black number, 1 to 12. Children are to work in small groups to draw the right number and kinds of things that the song suggests. (Make two sets to perform as stated above.)

1 partridge in a pear tree
2 turtledoves
3 French hens
4 calling birds
5 golden rings
6 geese a laying
7 swans a swimming
8 maids a milking
9 ladies dancing
10 lords a leaping
11 pipers piping
12 drummers drumming

Activity Center **A Wreath for the Door**

Place a large artificial evergreen wreath in the center with numerous small ornaments and green string. Have the children work in the center to decorate the wreath with as many ornaments as they can. Top it off with a large red bow and hang it on your door.

Make others for the helpers in your school—the principal, director, secretary, janitor, nurse, counselor, etc.

Activity Center **Glittering Stocking**

Place several different stocking-shaped patterns in the center. Allow each child to choose one from the stack, place it on a piece of plain wrapping paper, and trace around it with a pencil.

Make a wash of white glue and water. Have the children paint the stocking with the wash and then sprinkle glitter all over the stocking. When that is dry, have the children go around the edges with a string of white glue, and apply an outline of a second color of glitter. This will dry best if you can find a piece of old cardboard to tape the stocking to. Tape it around the edges with red or green tape.

Activity Center **What Shall I Give?**

On pieces of paper 4″ x 4″ (10.16 x 10.16 cm), have the children draw things that they would like to give other people. Glue the pictures above the glittering stocking that they made in the above activity.

Trees

Children are always interested in trees and certainly a study of trees is appropriate for the time in which we live. We need to be aware of what is in our environment, how to take care of it, and how to make sure that there will be trees in the future.

Trees for Life is a nonprofit organization developed specifically to help people in developing countries to plant and take care of trees. Write to them requesting information about trees. For a nominal fee ($12.50 plus shipping in 1990), they will send a teacher's workbook, seeds and a planting carton for each child (thirty children).

Trees for Life
1103 Jefferson
Wichita, KS 67203

Group Activity — **A Tree Walk**

Take the children on a walk around your school and look for trees. Try to determine whether they are evergreen/pine trees or leafing trees. Children can pick up tree parts from the ground to put on bulletin boards in the classroom.

Activity Center — **That Tree in the Window**

Provide for each child a 9" x 12" (22.86 x 30.48 cm) piece of white drawing paper, crayons and a view of the window. Let them draw a picture of the tree that they see through the window. Put a brown or black window frame around the picture and post on the bulletin board.

Activity Center **Splash Trees**

In a center near teacher supervision place 12″ x 18″ (30.48 x 45.72 cm) pieces of drawing paper, brown and black crayons, leaf-shaped sponges and paint for leaves. Change the color of the paint depending on the season.

Children can first sit at one half of the center where they draw the skeleton of the tree—the bare branches—with the brown crayon and color over it with black to make the texture of bark.

On the other side of the table provide the newspaper cover for the table, paint smocks and dishes of paint and leaf sponges. Children "splash" the tree full of color.

Activity Center **Leaf Trees**

An activity requiring leaves from trees is one that is good for fall or for when trees are pruned. Children need quite a collection of leaves to complete the task.

Provide a piece of old cardboard—a side of a box—for each child, glue and their leaves. A stick or piece of bark only from the ground can serve as the trunk of the tree. The leaves serve as themselves. Make a forest in the hall or let the trees go home.

Group Activity **Watch a Tree**

If you have a good tree outside your window, have the children observe the tree once a month—on the first or on payday so you can remember—and record what it looks like. Recording can take place in an eight to nine-page book or a piece of paper 19" x 4" (48.26 x 10.16 cm) folded into eight parts, each part numbered.

See if you see changes over a period of time. If you start in the fall and continue until spring, you should see some changes.

Group Activity **Where Are the Leaves?**

Give each child a paper sack. Go on an outdoor leaf hunt. Bring the leaves back into the classroom. Sort into like leaves. Group by categories.

Activity Center **Leaf Person**

After collecting the leaves and doing the activities, put them all together and use for nature collages, seed collages, leaf collages. Have the children try to make a leaf person by using a large leaf for the head and various sizes and shapes of leaves for the other body parts.

Activity Center **Leaf Rubbings**

Provide the children with several different leaves which have been flattened. Tape or glue the leaves to the table or a piece of paper. Give them various sizes of paper and have them place the paper on top of the leaf and tape it down. Using the side of unwrapped crayons, have the children make rubbings of the leaves. Use these in several different ways.

1. Tape the real leaf on one side of the paper and the rubbing on the other.
2. Cut out around the rubbed leaf and tape onto a blank bulletin board tree.
3. Label the tree/leaf at the bottom of the page. Staple several different ones together to make a book.

Black History Week
Martin Luther King, Jr.

Martin Luther King, Jr., was born in Atlanta, Georgia, on January 15, 1929, the son of a Baptist minister. His work for equal rights for all people and his nonviolent stance are important lessons even for young children. During the week in January when Black History Week is celebrated, the young children can focus on equal rights, nonviolent settlements and brotherhood.

Good Books for young children include
Martin Luther King, Jr., a Picture Story, Boone-Jones
Meet Martin Luther King, Jr., de Kay
If You Had Lived in the Times of Martin Luther King, Jr.

Activity Center **Sticking Together**

Place several pieces of 6" x 7" (15.24 x 17.78 cm) sheets of construction paper the shades of the skin of the children in your classroom. Try to get as many different shades of white, beige, tan, brown, black that you can. Have each child trace around his/her hand and cut the handprint out and write his/her name on the back.

Make a large bulletin board for storing the handprints. Children can stick them on the bulletin board in a circle, each hand holding another.

Activity Center **Friends Together**

Place large sheets of brown butcher paper in the center along with pencils, scissors and crayons.

Children are to work in pairs. One child lies facedown on the paper and assumes a position with hands at his sides. The other child traces around the first. They switch places and jobs. The two children then sit and chat while they cut themselves out and color themselves.

Place in the hallway under the words *Friends Together*. Make sure that the friends are holding hands.

Activity Center **I Have a Dream**

After reading about Martin Luther King Jr., and his dream of peace for the world, have the children write or draw pictures about how people could get along better. Record what the children have to say about their dreams. Post them on a dream cloud above the Friends Together or Sticking Together bulletin boards in the classroom.

Group Activity **Where in the World?**

Send home a note to parents asking them to list the name and birth place of their child and the names of the child's parents and grandparents.

Place a large map of the United States on the wall.

Give the children a blue marker to mark where they were born.

Give children red markers and have them put their names on the markers. Place the markers on the spots to mark where their parents were born.

Give children white markers and have them put their names on the markers. Place the markers on the spots where their grandparents were born.

Group Activity **Songs of the South**

Sing several of the Negro Spirituals that the children can easily learn—"We Shall Overcome," "My Old Kentucky Home," "Old Black Joe," We Are Climbing Jacob's Ladder."

Activity Center **Nice and Not Nice**

Provide the children with pencils, crayons and 12" x 18" (30.48 x 45.72 cm) sheets of paper folded in half.

Have each child draw a picture on one half of the paper that shows a nice way to ask for or get something. On the other half draw a picture of a way not to get something. Record what the children say at the bottom. Share the pictures in a large group. See the following group activity to see what to do next.

Group Activity **Nice and Not Nice**

Use the pictures from the preceding activity. Have the children tell about their pictures. As they tell about the pictures, record at the bottom what they say if you have not already. When they are finished, cut the picture in half and place all the pictures in one pile.

When all children have shared their pictures—which might be at the end of the week—make a happy face on one sheet of white paper and a sad face on the other. Place the happy face on the floor in front of you. Place the sad face next to it. Have each child tell about his picture and whether it goes in the Nice (happy face) pile or the Not Nice (sad face) pile.

After you have gone through the stack, place the pictures and faces in the following sorting center.

Activity Center **Making Decisions for Nice and Not Nice**

Use the pictures from the preceding Activity Center. After demonstrating the sorting process in the Group Activity above, children can work in pairs to decide just what stack to put the pictures in.

Tools

Little children are fascinated by tools they see used and ones that they are allowed to use. What better way to capture their imagination and critical thinking skills than capitalizing on this curiosity.

Safety
Stress the importance of following the rules when using tools. Show the children exactly how to use the tool, how to pick it up, how to return it to its place of keeping. Ask them to discuss what might happen if they didn't use the tool correctly.

Definition
The best way to distinguish a tool from a machine is for the children to learn the definition of a tool. A tool is an instrument we use with our hands for doing work, requiring no other energy.

Materials for Addition to the Standard Centers — **Using Tools**
Place additional tools in the kitchen area—spatulas, pancake flippers, plastic ware, wooden spoons.

Place additional tools in the outdoor equipment area—hoes, shovels, spades.

Measure with measuring tapes. Draw a picture of the object of distance measured and record the distance.

Group Motivating Activity — **What's in the Box?**
Fill a toolbox with a variety of tools. Present the toolbox to the children at circle time or place it on a "What's It?" table. Keep them guessing with "What do you think this is? What do you think might be in it? Where might you see one of these? What do you know about these types of things?"

Group Activity — **Music**
Sing "Johnny Works with One Hammer" and "John Henry Was a Steel Driving Man." Sing "This Is the Way We Hammer a Nail" to the tune of "Here We Go 'Round the Mulberry Bush."

Group Activities **Stories**

Read about John Henry and Paul Bunyan.

Other books about tools for young children are
We Help Daddy,
Mr. Bell's Fixit Shop,
The Toolbox

Activity Center **Paper Tool Hunt**

Have the children use catalogs and magazines to find pictures of tools. Have them cut them out and chart them, putting tools of like kinds in the same part of the chart.

Group Activity **Tools of the Trade**

Send home a note to the parents telling them that you are studying about tools in school this week. Ask each of them to send a "tool" of their trade to school with their child and to discuss with their child their job what they do on their job and how they use the tool.

Have each child tell about his parent's "tool of the trade" during a group activity time.

Activity Center **Where Does This Belong?**

Bring in tools such as a spatula, eggbeater, trowel, shovel, wrench, spoon, file, brush, etc. Let the children classify the tools in various ways.

Activity Center **Our Tools**

Go on a tool hunt in the room looking for classroom tools. Have the children name them. Make labels for the tools. Place the tools and labels in the handwriting center and provide paper, pencil and crayons to write the words.

Activity Center **Fill the Toolbox**

Fill a box with thirty nuts/bolts combinations and one die. Take all the nuts/bolts out of the box. Have one child roll the die and count out that number of nuts/bolts and place them in the box. The next child rolls and follows suit. The exact number must be rolled to take the last nut/bolt.

Activity Center **Guess How Many**

Give the children a plastic jar full of bolts. Have them guess how many are in the jar. Count them. Give them jars of different sizes and have them guess how many are in those.

Activity Center **Sifting**

Give children different sizes of sifters and coarse sand to sift and sort.

Activity Center **Mountains and Valleys**

Fill the water table with dirt. Give the children tools to make mountains and valleys. Be brave and try rivers with real water.

Activity Center **Making Food**

Have children make their own snacks using plastic knives, spoons, toothpicks, celery, peanut butter, cream cheese. Try these snacks:

Food		Tool
peanut butter	crackers	plastic knife
cream cheese	crackers	plastic knife
fruit salad	put different fruits in different bowls and let children spoon them into bowl	spoon
apple bits	cut apples into sections; have children cut into bite-sized pieces	table knife
yogurt/fruit	place in two bowls; let children spoon the two together	spoon

Okay, kids, now stir us together!
YOGU

Lincoln

Many patriotic holidays occur during the late spring and summer. Young children will not necessarily remember all of them or what they mean, but the more exposure they have to these holidays, the more they might mean later in life.

Presidents' Day is celebrated in February. Lincoln's birthday (February 12) and Washington's birthday (February 22) are both celebrated on Presidents' Day which is a Monday in February.

For further information about how to celebrate this and other holidays with young children, see *Learning About Fall & Winter Holidays* and *Learning About Spring & Summer Holidays,* Good Apple, Inc., 1988.

For young children the focus of study on patriotic holidays can be on

red, white, blue	the American flag
historical figures	civil rights
citizenship	American arts and crafts

For Lincoln, focus on his life and tie it to the objects in his life that start with the "L" sound.

Group Activity **Legend of the Groundhog**

Lincoln's birthday is February 12. We look for the groundhog on February 2. Study the legend of the groundhog. Look for shadows on February 2.

Group Activity **Local Library**

Lincoln loved to read. Take a trip to the local library.

Happy Birthday, President Lincoln!

Group Activity **Line Work**

Children can work cooperatively in an assembly line to make cherry tarts and blueberry tarts for snack.

Ingredients needed:

- cherry pie filling
- blueberry pie filling
- baked tart shells
- Cool Whip

The assembly line:

Have the children work on one side of a table, four in a line.

The first person is the tart giver.	Place the tart on a piece of waxed paper in front of the tart filler.
The second person is the tart filler.	Fill the tart with pie filling.
The third person is the tart decorator.	Decorate tart with Cool Whip.
The fourth is the tart placer.	Place tart on serving tray.

Serve with cranberry juice for snack.

Activity Center **Lanterns**

Make lanterns during the L week's celebration for Lincoln. Each child will need a 9" x 12" (22.86 x 30.48 cm) piece of red, white or blue construction paper; one 3" (7.62 cm) square of cardboard; one toilet paper roll and orange/yellow tissue paper.

Directions for the lantern:

Cut one 1" (2.54 cm) strip off the end of the 9" x 12" (22.86 x 30.48 cm) construction paper.
Put your name on the strip.
Save this for the handle of the lantern.
Fold the construction paper in half.
Use a ruler to mark a 1" (2.54 cm) line on the open end of the paper.
Use scissors to cut 1" (2.54 cm) strips from the fold to the marked line.
Open up.
Roll and staple the ends together to make a lantern.
Glue or staple the long strip saved earlier to the top to make a handle.

Directions for the candle:

Paint the toilet paper roll red, white or blue.
Fill the end with tissue paper.
Glue to the 3" (7.62 cm) piece of cardboard.

To assemble the lantern:

Put the lantern over the top of the candle.
Stand on shelf for display.

Activity Center **Locomotive**

Lincoln travelled across the country on a train. Make locomotives from precut black circles, rectangles, triangles and squares.

In the center put several pictures of train engines from the "olden days."

Place all the precut black construction paper there along with some glue. Let the children make locomotives.

Activity Center

Light and Heavy

During the study of L during Lincoln week, set up a discovery center where children can discover what is light and what is heavy.

Provide children with scales, objects and sacks for collecting objects to weigh that they can find in the classroom.

Older children can predict and record what they think is the heaviest by looking at it and then weighing and recording those results. The recording sheet is simple.

Light	Heavy	Right	Wrong

Activity Center

Shadows

Draw a picture of Lincoln with crayons on a piece of 12" x 18" (30.48 x 45.72 cm) paper, turned the tall way, of course. After the picture is colored, cut it out. Place it on a piece of black paper. Trace around it. Cut out Lincoln's shadow. Post on the bulletin board by putting the black one up first and the colored picture slightly off the edge of the black one. If you are daring, let the children stand their colored Lincoln up by glueing it to a paper towel tube and laying the black shadow on the countertop in back of the colored picture.

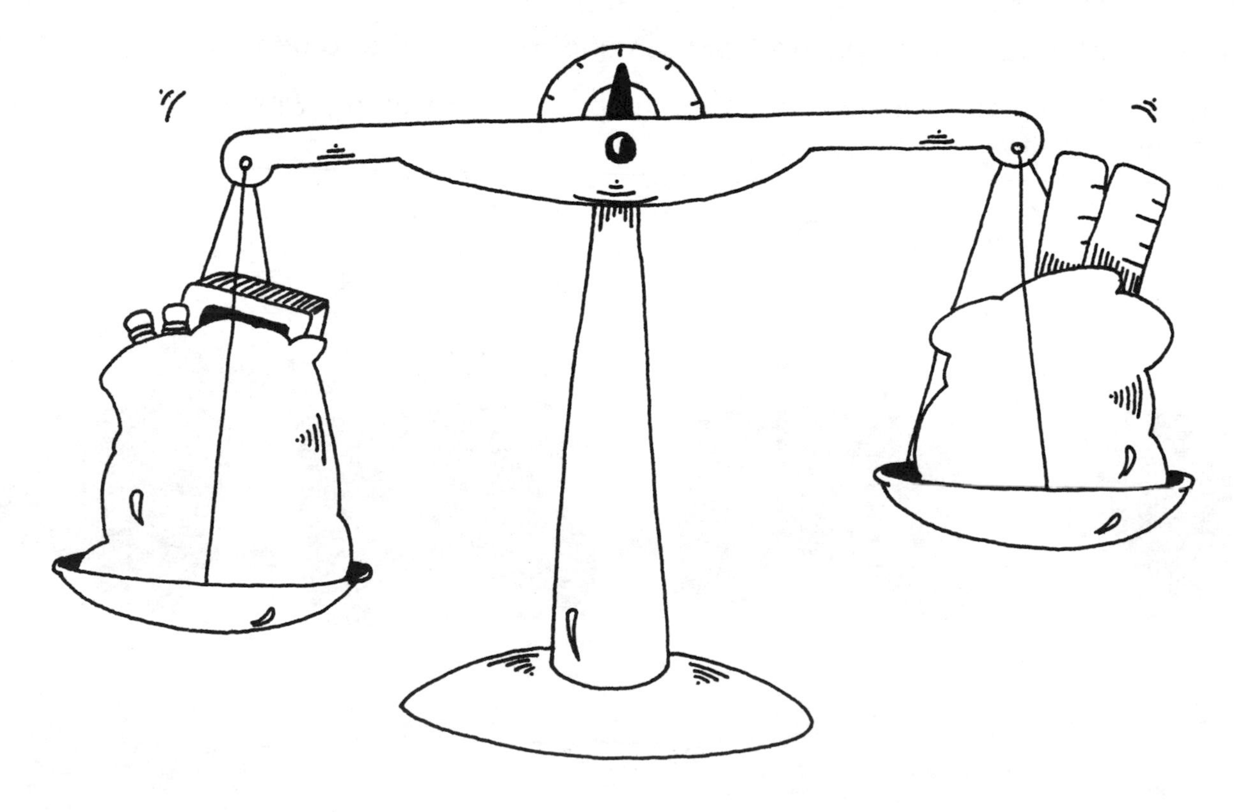

Insects

Spring and summer are good times to explore the world of the insects. Children's reactions to bugs vary. Some are fearless, picking up any of the bugs that cross their paths. These children need to develop some skills for identifying those insects that are dangerous and should not be bothered. Some children are frightened of any small thing moving. These children need some skills to identify those that are harmless, helpful and fun to watch.

Insects have certain characteristics that identify them as insects.

1. The insect has three separate body parts or sections. The parts are called the head, the thorax and the abdomen and are in that order on the body.
2. Each insect has six legs (three pairs) for walking. Some of the insects have one pair of legs that are longer than the others and they use these for jumping.
3. Each insect has two pairs of wings. This doesn't mean that all insects can fly. Some of these wings do not allow the insect to fly. Some insects are not equipped to fly.
4. The insect has a hard outer shell that protects the inner parts of the insect's body.
5. The insect has a pair of antennae at the top of the head. These antennae help guide the insect's flight much the same as a radio antennae does by receiving messages and telling the insect by sound and motion what is around it.

Some insects you and your children might want to examine are the housefly, beetle, ladybug, bee, dragonfly and the mosquito.

Some insects are harmful to man. Grasshoppers and locusts destroy crops. Gypsy moths destroy our shade trees. Termites eat through wooden buildings. Carpet beetles do damage in homes. Clothes moths make holes in our clothes.

Spiders are not insects. Spiders have eight legs.

Group Activity **Bugs in a Bottle**

Bring in an insect in a bottle for the children to observe. Grasshoppers are great for this. They are harmful to us but not dangerous to the children. Place the grasshopper in a large bottle with a lid that allows for air to get to the insect. Place fresh grass in the bottle each time the grass dies. Be sure to add a drop or two of water daily.

Let children examine the insect with the bare eyes and with a magnifying glass and tell you something about what they see. After the children have told you what they see, ask questions about the visible properties that they have not mentioned.

Group Activity **So Small, So Tall!**

Let the children work in pairs. One child stands up tall. The other gets down on all fours and hops from place to place. Let the grasshopper look up at the one standing. See how tall "he" looks. How does that grasshopper feel?

Group Activity **Bug Walk**

Take the children on a bug walk to collect bugs. Take along a bug bottle/bug catcher. Each child can make his own using a baby food jar, a piece of netting and a rubber band. To catch bugs with this bottle, place the bottle over the bug, slide a piece of 4" x 4" (10.16 x 10.16 cm) tagboard under the jar and bug. Turn the jar over allowing the bug to drop to the bottom of the jar. Put in some twigs and grass. Place the netting over the bottle and attach with a rubber band.

Activity Center **Let's Find Out**

Materials:

- several books about insects
- a sheet of paper
- crayons
- pencils

Write *Insects* at the top of the page.

Find pictures of grasshoppers in the books.

Look at the number of the page and write the number of the page on your piece of paper. Draw a picture of the grasshopper you see on that page or write something that it says about the grasshopper.

Activity Center **Bugs in a Bottle**

Materials:

- construction paper
- white drawing paper
- crayons
- scissors
- pencils

Cut out a large bottle shape from white butcher paper and write at the top of the bulletin board *Bugs in a Bottle*.

Have the children draw pictures of grasshoppers with their pencils, color the grasshoppers the colors they know grasshoppers to be, cut out the grasshoppers, place their names on the back and pin their grasshoppers in the large bottle on the bulletin board.

Activity Center **My Bug Bottle**

Have the children make a two-dimensional bug bottle. Provide them with a bottle shape. Have them trace around the bottle onto a piece of tagboard. Cut out the tagboard-shaped bottle. Cut out the center of the bottle within 1″ (2.54 cm) of the edges. Tape clear plastic wrap to make the bottle. As they draw bugs, have them glue or tape them to the plastic wrap. Hang in the windows.

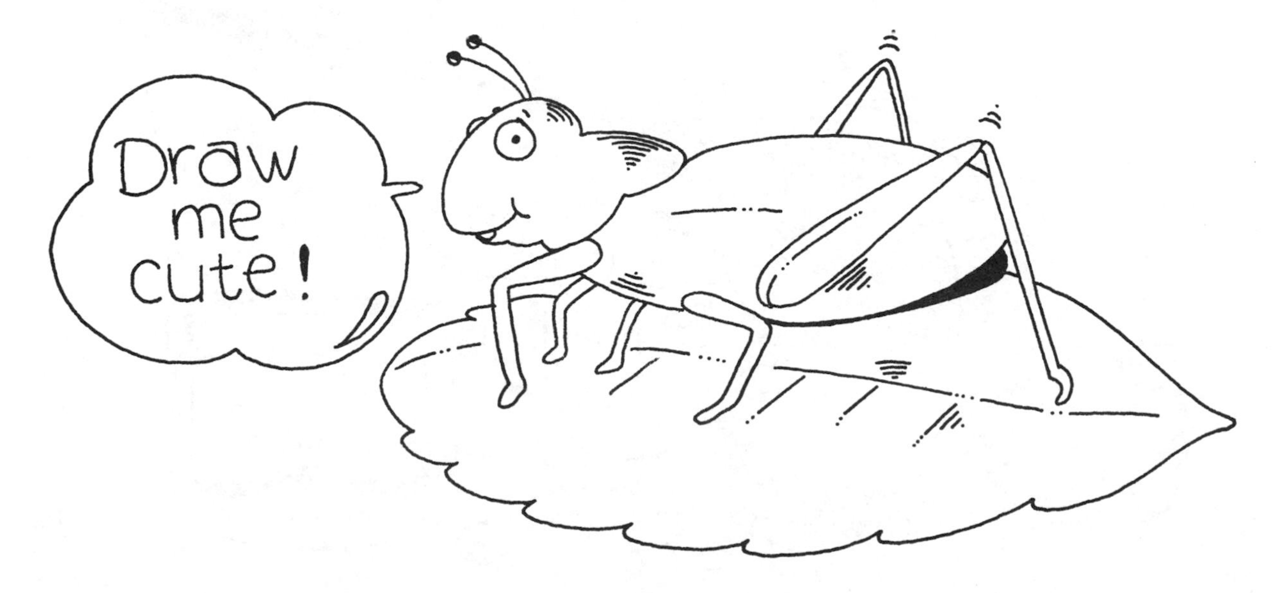

Activity Center **Other Bugs**

Provide a variety of materials for children to make bugs of their choice. Place them in the bug bottle on the bulletin board.

Activity Center **Bug Collecting**

Provide pictures of various kinds of insects in the center. Let children draw pictures of the insects to put in their own bug bottles which they make at the center described on the preceding page.

Activity Center **Anatomy of an Insect**

Materials to be provided by the teacher in the center:

- drawing of an insect with labelled parts
- ditto of same insect without labelled parts
- pencils

Children are to look at the drawing of the insect where the parts are labelled.

Copy the names of the parts from the drawing onto your paper.

Count the number of each part and write that number next to the name of the part.

Activity Center **Pair Up for Butterflies**

Provide the children with a cutout butterfly, black tempera and brushes, wet pieces of sponges and bright colors of dry tempera. Have them fold it in half. Each pair of children completes two butterflies. Children take the first butterfly. One student is the leader. The follower repeats whatever the leader does on the other half of the butterfly. The leader dabs one color of paint in a spot or two. The follower follows. Complete until the leader is satisfied. The pair then changes places. The follower becomes the leader, the leader the follower. Children make a second butterfly.

When the butterflies are dry, each leader gets the butterfly made when he was leader, and using black tempera colors around the edges. Older children can then fine-line with black paint and thin brushes around the colors.

Rocks

Children love to play with, explore, hunt for and in general find out about rocks. They are easy to find, especially ones of your particular area. Try some of these activities to excite them about their environment. Connect the study of rocks to Plymouth Rock and the Pilgrims or to some of the fine books for young children.

Group Activity **Sylvester and the Magic Pebble**

Read the story about Sylvester and the Magic Pebble to the children and have a pebble close by to show them when Sylvester finds his. Show the children the different sizes of rocks in the pictures of the book. As a group, children can paint two large pieces of wadded up white butcher paper gray, staple the edges, stuff with newspaper and put on the bulletin board for the beginning of a rock bulletin board.

Group Activity **Gathering Pebbles**

Take the children outside with collection bags. (Baggies are best because they can see through them, but you can use small paper sacks. Be sure to let each child put his/her name on the bag. If children use Baggies, have them put their name on a card in the Baggie.) Collect all the pebbles, rocks and stones that the children can carry.

Activity Center **Where Did I Get These Rocks?**

When the children return to the room, have them put their pebbles in a special spot. At a center place 12″ x 18″ (30.48 x 45.72 cm) sheets of paper and some crayons. Children are to draw things that they saw on their trip outside and the rocks that they found.

Group Activity **This Is How I Got My Rocks**

When students have drawn their maps, use one or two and a stick puppet to show how the puppet walks the path and picks up the rocks. Have the children do it with stick puppets on their own (clothespins will do). After they have followed the path, have them draw the path using their black crayon as the puppet. They will then have a map.

Activity Center **Sorting Pebbles**

Place three sheets of white paper about 6" x 12" (15.24 x 30.48 cm) in the center for each child. Children sort their pebble collection into two groups and share with another person at the center the characteristics they have used to sort their rocks.

Each child takes an additional sheet of paper and rearranges his/her rocks into three groups. Have the children chat with their partners about the characteristics they have now used to sort their rocks.

Activity Center **Graphing the Pebbles**

Make individual graphs for each child on a piece of paper with 1" (2.54 cm) squares. Use the graph for many, many things. Place the blank paper in the center. Have the child choose one of his rocks and put it at the bottom of the graph. See how many other rocks there are of that size or color and put them in the boxes above the first rock. Continue to see which rocks have the most.

Activity Center **Weighing the Rocks**

Let the children weigh the rocks on some balance scales and see how many of one kind of rock it takes to make the same weight as another kind of rock. You needn't tell them what to do. Demonstrate two or three times how they might weigh without ever saying a word, just using a curious facial expression.

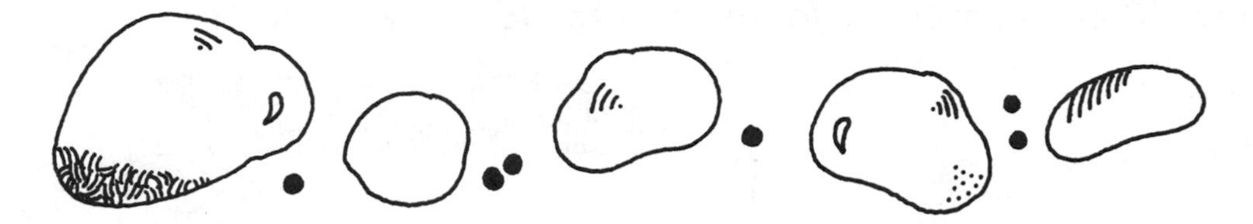

Activity Center **Down to the Last Rock**

Put twenty rocks in a margarine container. Place it in a Ziploc bag with a meat tray from the butcher. Also place one die or a spinner in the Baggie.

Let two children play the game. Put all the rocks in the meat tray. Have one child (the youngest for the first game and the oldest for the second game) roll the die. That child takes that many rocks out of the tray and puts them into the margarine container. The second child rolls and does the same, each child checking the other.

When they get down to the last few rocks, the exact number must be taken, but they keep taking turns until the last rock is taken. Don't keep track of winners/ losers. Just have them say "We did it!" and do it again.

Activity Center **Sifting Sand**

Find various sizes of sifters. Have the children place their rocks and pebbles in the sifters to see if any fall through the holes. See if they can tell you why some do and why some do not fall through.

Activity Center **Pet Rocks**

Have each child pick a favorite rock to make into a pet rock. Let them paint the rocks. Let them dry. Paint features on the rocks. Let them dry. Have the children make houses for the rocks out of small boxes or folded paper boxes.

Have children dictate to you how to take care of their pet rocks and write those directions down. Send them home for the children to take care of.

Activity Center **How Many Rocks?**

Have the children take one handful of rocks and glue them to a strip of adding machine tape lengthwise. Under each rock, have the children write the numbers 1-9 (or however many they have). Post these for all children to see. They will begin to notice the sizes and the numbers.

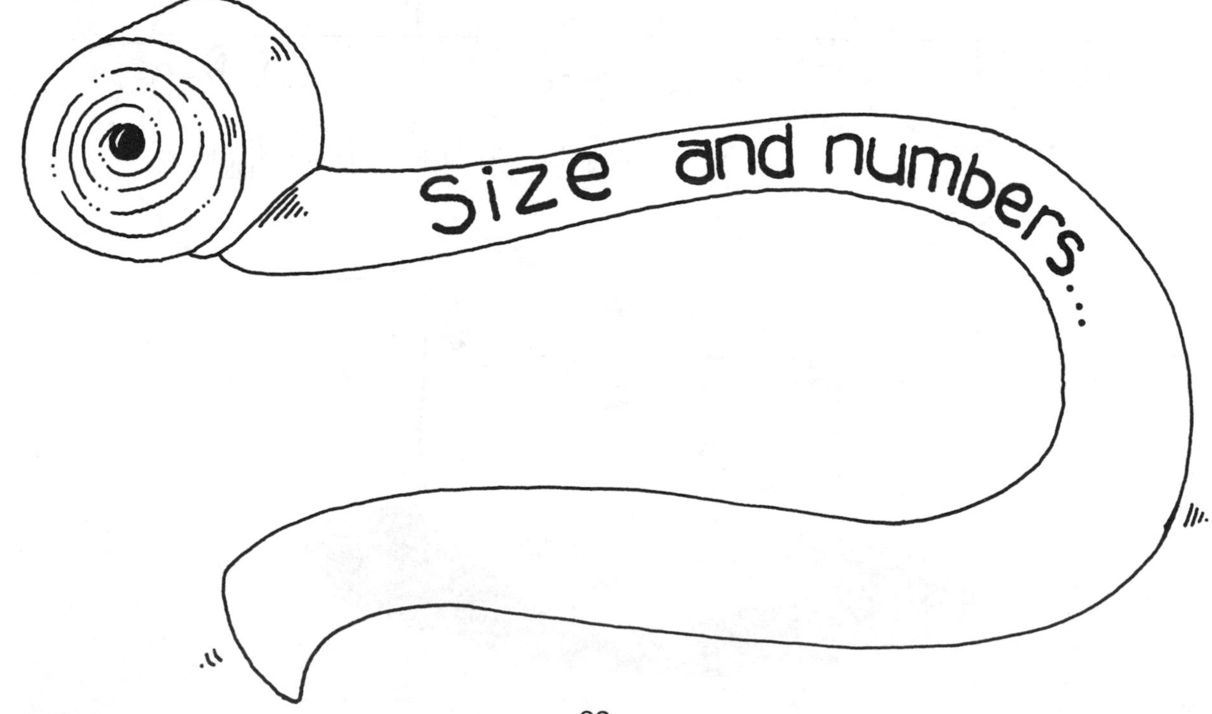

St. Patrick's Day

St. Patrick's Day happens in early spring. It is a great time not only to celebrate the day but the comin' of the green. Focus on green activities as well as have some fun with the leprechauns.

Two other Good Apple books contain ideas for St. Patrick's Day and green. Try *Learning About Spring & Summer Holidays* (1988) and *The Complete Color Book* (1991).

Culminating Bulletin Board **Postin' of the Green**

As the children do the activities in this unit, post them on the bulletin board. Make sure that most things are green and that each shows something made of a different texture of material.

Activity Center **Glittery Shamrocks**

Place several small shamrock patterns in the center for the children to trace on white paper.

Have them cut out the shamrocks and cover with a thin coat of glue. Sprinkle with green glitter—remember after Christmas next year to buy some on sale to save for now. Let children take some home, save one for wearin' on St. Patrick's Day and put some on the Postin' of the Green bulletin board.

Activity Center **Patchy Shamrocks**

Place several small shamrock patterns in the center for the children to trace on white paper.

Have them cut out the shamrocks and cover with a thin coat of glue. Place several different shades of green artist tissue paper in the center in 1″ (2.54 cm) squares. Have children pick up the squares and place them on the shamrock, overlapping to make darker shades, but not going over the edges any more than necessary. They can cut off the edges when dry, if necessary.

Activity Center **Little Leprechauns**

Show children pictures of leprechauns. Point out the hats, belts, jackets, shoes and the unique faces.

Leave pictures of leprechauns in this center. Have the children draw pictures on various sizes of leprechauns for the Postin' of the Green bulletin board.

Group Activity **Growin' of the Green**

Get a long trough-type plastic wallpaper tray to use as a planter. Put some gravel in the bottom. Add soil. Sprinkle grass seed along the top. Put another bit of dirt on the top.

Water as necessary. Place the planter at the base of the bulletin board so the grass grows up at the bottom of it.

Activity Center **Readin' of the Green**

Provide blank books at this center. Make them by folding four sheets of 4¼" x 5½" (10.76 x 13.95 cm) sheets of paper in half. When closed, fold the fold over ½" (1.25 cm) and staple on that fold.

Have children draw a different green thing on each page. Put a green cover on the book made from a 6" x 12" (15.24 x 30.48 cm) piece of green construction paper and title it *The Green Book*.

Writin' of the Green

To make it a fine reading activity, write a simple language pattern throughout the book as the children tell you what they have drawn. Try A ______________ is green. This is a green ______________. See the green ______________.

Put them in the library for the children to read at their leisure. Post one on the bulletin board.

Post another in a green book bag that the leprechaun can carry.

Activity Center **Tastin' of the Green**

Place celery, green pepper, lettuce, green onions, fresh cooked green beans in the center. Provide seriated table knives, green paper plates and green napkins for the children.

Let the children cut the vegetables into small pieces and place a few on their green plates to eat for a snack. Top it off with green paper cups and lime Kool-Aid for a drink.

Group Activity **Wearin' of the Green**

Send home a note to the parents asking that the children wear green on St. Patrick's Day. The class will look great.

Group Activity **Sharin' of the Green**

Send home a note to the parents asking that the children bring something green from their home for the Sharin' of the Green on the same day that they will be Wearin' of the Green.

Group Activity **Runnin' with the Green**

On St. Patrick's Day set up relays for the children. Divide the children into two to three teams. Split the teams in half. Put half at one end of the room and the others at the other end of the room.

Give the leader of the team a spoonful of a green Jell-O cube. Have them run to the other end of the relay area and give the spoonful of Jell-O to their team member at the other end. That person then passes the spoonful of Jell-O to their team member, etc. Let them do it for three minutes and call time. Do not have a winner.

Hats

What fun hats are for children to try on! Spring is a good time to study about hats because of St. Patrick's Day, rain hats, Easter hats and the wind. Make hats the theme for a couple of weeks and try these activities. You can focus on some fine fun reading also. These books are good starters:

Good Books to Read

Jennie's Hat
A Three-Hat Day
Who Stole the Farmer's Hat?
Word Bird's Hats
Caps for Sale

Group Activity **Hat Day**

Ask the parents to send a child's hat with the children to leave at school for the week. In addition, have each child bring one hat representing each member of his/her family. You will end up with all kinds of hats. Be sure to label the hats with the name of the child who brought them. A safety pin and a piece of paper work best.

Activity Center **Sorting Hats (Read *A Three-Hat Day*)**

After all the hats have arrived, place them in a center and have the children generate the labels for the types and place that label at the bottom of a column and put hats of that type in one column. Graph the hats on a graph made from 1′ (.304 m) segments on an old tarp. Types of hats might include winter hats, straw hats, baseball caps, sailor hats, helmets, bonnets, cowboy hats, beanies, etc.

When this sorting hat task is done, give each child a pencil, crayons and 3″ x 5″ (7.62 x 12.7 cm) index cards. Encourage children to look at the graph on the floor and find the hats that they brought from home. Have each write the name of the type of hat(s) he brought on the front of the 3″ x 5″ card and draw a picture of it on the back of the 3″ x 5″ card. Make a new card for each hat. Place these writing cards in a writing center where children may use them for writing.

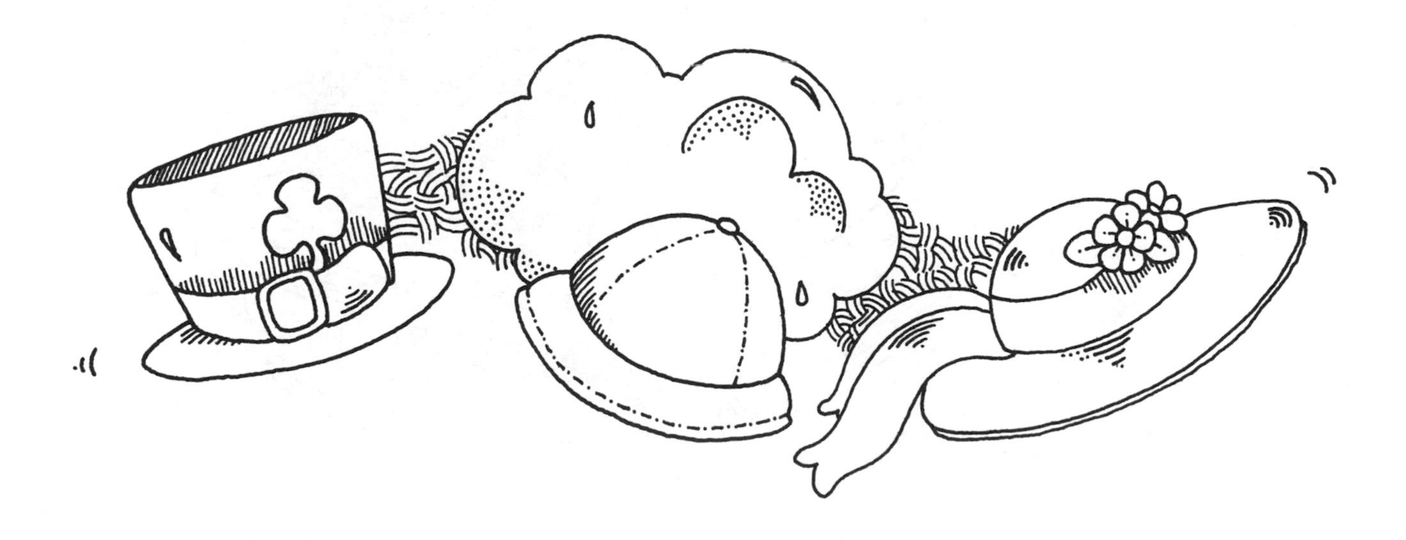

Group Activity **Hats and Jobs (Read *Word Bird's Hat*)**

Have each child select a hat that he/she brought to school that might show a kind of job that someone does. As children share their hats with the group, they can tell what type of hat it is, who might wear it, and what the person wearing it might do. For example:

"This is a helmet. It might be worn by a football player of the Minnesota Vikings."

Activity Center **How Much Does It Weigh?**

Let children weigh the hats brought in on a balance scale. Have them put pennies on one side of the scale and the hat on the other side of the scale. When the children judge that the scale balances, have them take out the pennies and count how many pennies their hats weigh. They can record their results on a sheet.

Hat	Pennies
This hat weighs the same as ______ pennies.	

Activity Center **Hat Catalog**

Place catalogs of hats in this center with individual blank books for the children. These blank books are nothing more than several sheets of paper stapled together to make a book. If you want to get fancy, make the sheets hat-shaped.

Have the children cut out or draw pictures of hats, label them and place a cost on them. The cost can be real or from the children's knowledge of money.

Activity Center **Go Togethers (Read *Who Stole the Farmer's Hat?*)**

Have the children work in pairs. Each child is to pick out two hats from the hat stack that he thinks might go together. For example:

Two ski masks might go together because they are the same type.

A top hat and a fancy hat might go together because the people might go together to the ball.

Culminating Activity **Hat Parade**

After the children have made their hats and/or brought them from home, have a hat parade through your building. You may use a tape player for music or sing an appropriate song for the parade.

Wallpaper hats are great fun (see *Faces, Legs, and Belly Buttons*, Good Apple, 1984, page 50 for complete instructions and illustrations).

Basically you need two pieces of 18″ to 20″ (45.72 x 50.80 cm) squares of paper. Make a wash of glue and water and paste the two sheets together. Place the paper on the top of a head and shape it down around the head. Place a large rubber band around the head and let the child wear it around for a while. After a while cut the rubber band and take the hat off the head to dry. It will retain its shape. Let the children decorate the hats. Give them feathers, ribbon, glue, scissors, rickrack, artificial flowers or make tissue paper flowers (see *Faces, Legs, and Belly Buttons,* Good Apple, 1984, page 15 for complete instructions and illustrations). Try using only certain colors if you use the hat unit during a certain holiday—green for St. Patrick's Day, red, white or blue for the Fourth, pastels for Easter, red and green for Christmas, etc.

(Printer's hat, coonskin cap, soldier's hat, cook's hat, tall hat are all in *Faces, Legs, and Belly Buttons*, also.)

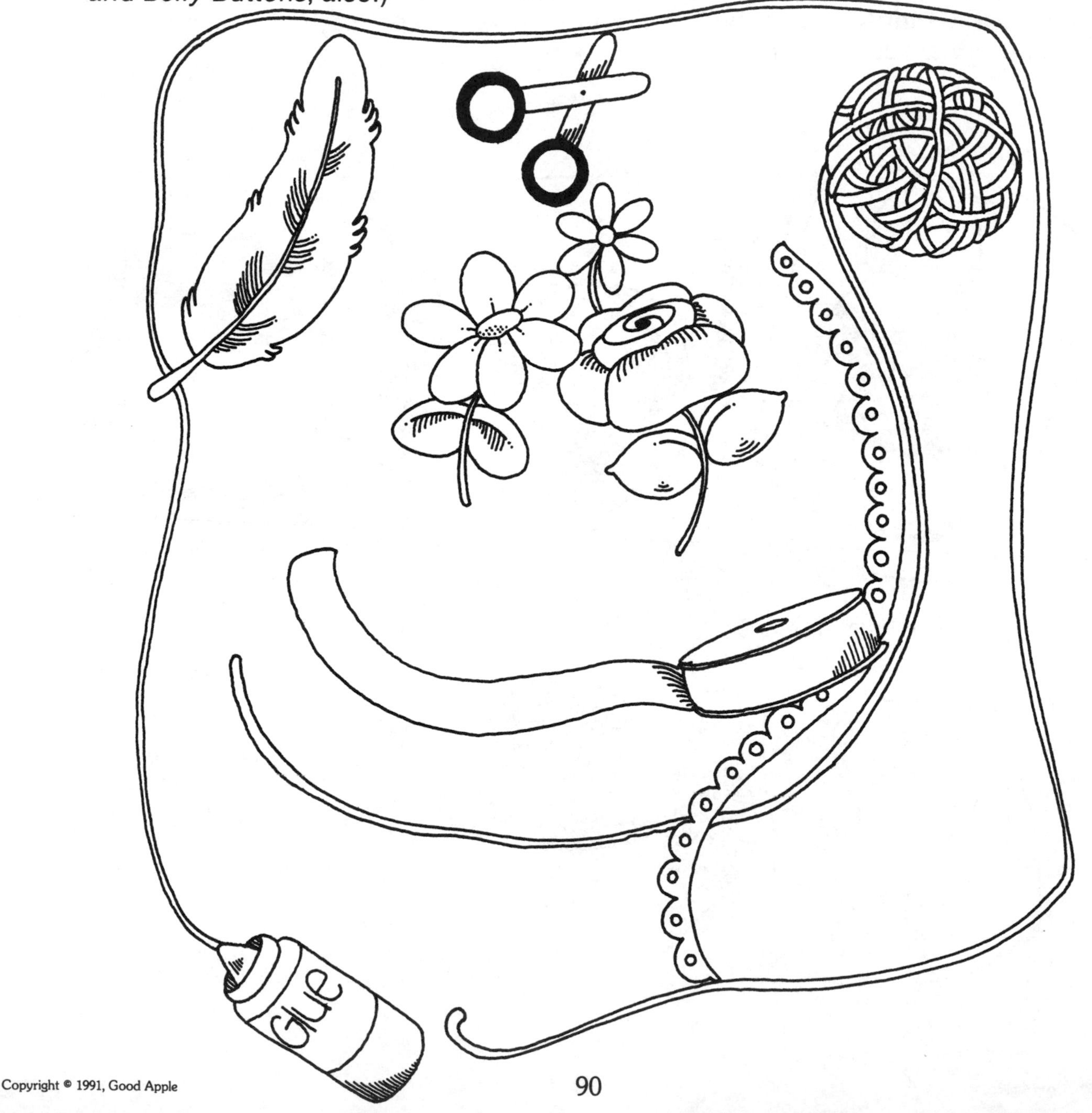

Easter

Ideas that are presented here are for those of you who can celebrate Easter and for those of you who cannot. Easter announces the coming of spring and the ideas here are for use with that coming.

Activity Center **Writing Easter (Spring) Words**

Place several children's dictionaries in the center along with pencils, crayons and 6″ x 6″ (15.24 x 15.24 cm) sheets of paper.

Demonstrate to the children how they can look at the pictures in the dictionaries in order to find pictures of things that they think about or see at Easter (in the spring). When they find a picture they then write the word at the bottom of the piece of paper and draw a picture on the sheet of paper.

Save these to put on a bulletin board of Easter (spring) words.

Group Activity **Nature Walk**

Give each child four to five index cards and a pencil.

Take the children on a nature walk to find the new signs of spring—buds, flowers, sprouts, etc. When they find something, have them sit down and write the name of what they see or draw a picture. When they see the first thing and draw it, put a #1 on the back, etc. (Record for yourself on a chart what they have seen/ written. When they return to the room, you can post the words and pictures for those who could not write the name while in the field.)

Post these on a bulletin board entitiled "Natural Signs of Spring."

Activity Center **Sorting Eggs**

Fill several pairs of plastic eggs with various small objects. Make sure that at least one pair of eggs has the same objects (use plastic and/or metal paper clips, small beads, buttons, jacks, marbles, small rubber balls, M & M's). Place all of these eggs in a basket with an egg carton nearby.

Children are to sort the eggs and find matches by listening to the sounds that they make and place them in the egg carton in pairs. When they have completed the task, they may check their responses by opening the eggs and checking them, at first leaving them in their right slot in the carton for a partner to check.

After the partner has checked the eggs, the child is to dump all objects into the lid of the carton and the final task is to place the same number and same objects back into each pair of the egg halves, have the teacher check them, eat the M & M's, and then put the eggs back together.

Activity Center **Egg Painting**

Have the children bring or provide children with blown eggs, pastel acrylic paint, brushes and paint smocks. Let them paint the eggs. Send home in milk carton egg baskets.

Activity Center **Egg Roll**

Cut out several 8" (20.32 cm) or larger egg-shaped pieces of paper. Decorate them as Easter eggs. On the back of each, put a number 1, 2 or 3. Place them in a basket along with several hard-boiled eggs of two colors or some plastic eggs or two colors filled with rubber balls, an egg-shaped scoring card and pencils. Children work in this center in pairs.

Demonstrate to the children how they should place the paper eggs number-side down on the carpet in various spots within a confined area. They then sit behind a piece of tape and roll the eggs toward the egg-shaped pieces of paper. Each of the eggs that their egg touches becomes their egg. At the end of the roll, they pick up their eggs, turn over the paper egg, record the number on the back of their scoring card, return their eggs to the basket, add up their number of points and compare it to their partners, circling the higher number.

Play again.

Activity Center **Egg Salad Sandwiches**

Provide the children with a recipe card that shows 1 egg, 1 tsp. (5 ml) mayonnaise, 2 pieces of bread, margarine.

Demonstrate how to peel the egg, use a fork to mash the egg, add 1 tsp. mayonnaise, spread margarine on one slice of bread, spread egg salad on the same slice, put the two slices together and put into Ziploc bag for snack later. (If children can eat it immediately, use crackers.)

Activity Center **Edible Easter Basket**

Let each child make individual edible baskets with edible eggs.

Cut a Twinkie in half the long way. Lay open. Place green coconut (shake coconut in a Ziploc Baggie with two drops of green food coloring) and jelly beans in the white filling to make them look like Easter baskets. Enjoy for a snack right before children go home.

Group Activity — **Field Trip**

Take a field trip to a local hatchery, children's zoo or small farm to see the babies. Let children see, touch, smell and hear the living sights and sounds of spring.

Activity Center — **Painted Eggs**

Cut egg shapes from slices of bread.

Make egg-yoke paint by letting the children separate the yoke from the white through their fingers. Place the yokes in a small bowl and add food coloring. Paint the bread. Toast.

Activity Center — **Egg Animals**

Provide the children with plastic eggs, permanent markers, glue, glitter, construction paper and scissors. Have them make animals (turtles, bunnies, chicks, dinosaurs) out of their eggs or egg halves. (Some suggestions are in the 1989 March/April issue of *Lollipops.*)

Seeds and Leaves

Seeds and leaves are objects that easily evoke interest in young children, they are accessible to teachers, and they are inexpensive as objects for learning. Leaves are available in the spring, summer and fall in most areas and even in the winter in others. Seeds are available in the fall and spring in the out-of-doors, and at garden and farm supply companies throughout the year.

Children will learn to recognize and name, sort, classify, observe, predict and inquire as they work with this unit.

In addition to lots of seeds and leaves for this unit, you will need many containers of various sizes, collecting bags, waxed paper, an iron and blank books.

Good Books to Read

The New True Books (*Plants We Know, Plants Without Seeds, Plant Experiments, Trees, Weeds and Wild Flowers)*
How Flowers Live
The Tiny Seed
A Tree Is Nice
Life-Cycle Books (*Flowers, Trees)*

Group Motivating Activity **Seed Hunt**

Take a trip to the grocery either with the children or before beginning the unit. Gather all kinds of fruits and vegetables.

During circle time provide an apple for an object lesson. Have the children describe the fruit by what they can see with the apple as a whole. Cut a slice off of the edge without entering the center seed pocket. Continue the description. Slice through the middle. Continue the description. Take out all of the seeds and set them in a margarine lid for observation on a science table. Taste and eat the apple for the conclusion of circle time.

Group Activity **Where Are the Seeds?**

Give each child a paper sack. Go on an outdoor seed hunt. Bring the seeds back to the classroom. Sort into like seeds. Group by categories—double winged, single winged, feathery, soft tufts, nuts, encased in pods.

Group Activity **Plant a Pair**

Gather a pair of large mismatched socks from your laundry basket. Let the children take turns wearing them in the grass at recess during the late fall or early spring. Plant them in a large container of dirt. Place in the sun. Water a little each day. Wait for the "socks" to grow.

Activity Center **Seed Hunt**

Place the other fruit and vegetables on a table for a seed hunt. Let the children use magnifying glasses to look for seeds in the fruits and vegetables. Have them draw pictures of the fruits/vegetables and their seeds. Post near the center.

Activity Center **Bags of Seeds**

Request a small amount (1 tsp.) (5 ml) of various types of seeds from a feed store. Store them in 2" x 3" (5.08 x 7.62 cm) Ziploc plastic bags. Let the children examine with magnifying glasses, a microscope and with their eyes and try to guess what types of plants will grow from the seeds. (Get two of each type and let them match the seeds.)

Activity Center **Seed Dig**

Provide scissors, spoons, plastic knives and fruit/vegetables for the children. Let them dig the seeds out of the produce. Save in one master cup.

Activity Center **What Seed Is This?**

Let the children sort them into small paper cups and try to find and label the fruit or vegetable from which it came.

Activity Center **Seed Collage**

Use the seeds gathered from outside and extras from the feed stores to make collages. From the seeds gathered from outside, the children can form the center of a picture of a flower from which they came or glue to a picture of a tree from which they came.

Activity Center **Planting Seeds**

Model for the children and then let them plant seeds. Try one of these methods.

1. Place a piece of sponge in water. Let it get thoroughly wet. Dab it in a container of grass seed. Place it in a pan of shallow water. Put in the sun.
2. Place a few rocks in the bottom of a cup. Put in soil. Place seeds across the top. Cover with soil. Lightly pack. Water. Place in the sun. Observe.
3. Cut off the top of a potato. Dig it out a bit. Place grass seed in the top.

Activity Center **Seed and Leaf Match**

Match the leaf and seed of the tree—maple leaf, maple seed; oak leaf, oak seed; elm leaf, elm seed. Have the children make a rubbing of the tree bark, glue the leaf to the paper, and then add the seed.

Activity Center **The Whole Tree**

Take a strip of paper 6" x 18" (15.24 x 45.72 cm). Fold into fourths. In the first fourth write the name of the plant. In the second make a rubbing of the trunk, stem or flower. In the third glue a leaf. In the fourth glue a seed. Do this with pinecones and pine needles, too. (Soak the pinecone in water and see what happens.)

Group Activity **What We Learned**

Make a class booklet of all of the various types of plants you have in your area. Individual children may make books of their own. Take the books to another classroom and "read" them to the other students.

Mother's Day
Father's Day

Mother's Day usually comes within the school year and Fathers are left out. Most of these activities can be modified to fit the fathers in your school. Send home the Father's Day gifts at the end of school so the children can save them until Father's Day. If you are in a year-round school, do the activities near Father's Day.

Group Activity **Mother's Day Tea**

Invite the mothers in for a Mother's Day tea during or right after the lunch hour. Let the children act out one of their favorite stories for the mothers, and then have a tea party of cookies that the children have made and a simple pineapple juice and 7-Up punch. Have the children give them gifts and cards from any of those listed below.

(For Father's Day make it a brunch or coffee to be held first thing in the morning. Serve juice and the Bisquick Velvet Crumb Cake which the children can make the day before.)

Activity Center **I Love Mom; I Love Dad**

Place patterns of 6" (15.24 cm) hearts in the center of red paper 7" x 7" (17.78 x 17.78 cm). Let the children trace around the hearts and cut them out of the red paper. On a 3" x 3" (7.62 x 7.62 cm) piece of paper each child can draw a picture of his/her face and glue it to the center of the heart. Around the top edge write *I Love Mom* or *I Love Dad*. Around the bottom edge write the child's name. (If you have pictures of the children, have these placed in the center of the hearts.)

Activity Center **Spicy Hearts**

Pink several heart shapes from small 4" x 4" (10.16 x 10.16 cm) pieces of printed material and plain material. Have the children do a simple stitch about ½" (1.25 cm) in from the edge starting about ½" (1.25 cm) from the center top of the heart and going until they reach the same point on the other side of the heart. Keep the needle threaded.

Fill the heart with spices—chunks of stick cinnamon or cedar chips—that cannot leak through the edges the children have sewn.

Finish the stitching.

Put a 6" (15.24 cm) piece of ¼" (.6 cm) ribbon in a loop at the top of the heart to hang.

Activity Center **Kitchen Goodies**

Make a recipe chart that contains the directions for this kitchen spice:

1 T. (15 ml) white pepper
1 T. (15 ml) garlic powder
1 T. (15 ml) salt
4 T. (60 ml) onion powder
6 T. (90 ml) parsley

Measure each of the above into the bowl. Mix it together well. Place a funnel in one baby food jar. Spoon 12 tablespoons (180 ml) into the top of the funnel. Put the lid on the jar. Tie a bow around the top of the jar near the lid.

Have children work in pairs to share the task.

Mix small amounts in sour cream or mayonnaise for dips or salads.

Activity Center **Bookmark**

Place several blank oaktag-weight strips of paper 2″ x 8″ (5.08 x 20.32 cm) in the center with ink pads. Have the children decorate a strip with their fingerprints.

Laminate the strips and send home as gifts.

Activity Center **Refrigerator Magnets**

Buy several different-shaped wooden pieces at the hobby store—hearts, umbrellas, cows, pigs, rainbows.

Have the children color these to decorate them, pressing hard with their crayons.

Place a piece of paper over the colored wooden piece and press with a hot iron.

Put a piece of magnetic tape on the back to cover as much of the wood as possible.

Send home as a gift.

Activity Center **What Do Moms Do All Day?**
What Do Dads Do All Day?

Place several blank books in the center, one for each child. Make them from four 8½″ x 11″ (21.6 x 27.94 cm) sheets of paper folded in half and stapled on the outside.

On each sheet have the children draw a picture of something their mom (dad) does each day. If they can write, have them write what it is. If not, have them dictate to you what they have drawn.

Make a cover from a piece of light-colored construction paper.

Have children draw pictures of their moms (dads) on pieces of 5″ x 8″ (12.7 x 20.32 cm) drawing paper, cut out and glue to the front.

Activity Center **From the Bottom of My Sole**

Measure the foot of the child who has the longest foot to determine what length of paper you will need to complete this card for Mother's Day (Father's Day). Add 2" (5.08 cm) to that length and make the cards that high. Make them wide enough to get the child's footprint in the center of the card.

Paint the child's foot with a paintbrush the color that he/she chooses from the selection of paints. Print the foot on the piece of paper.

On the inside of the card have each child write *I love you, Mom* (*I love you, Dad*) and sign his name.

Activity Center **Chip off the Old Block**

Give the children scraps of wood to sand. After it is smooth, let them oil the pieces of wood.

Glue a picture of the child on the piece of wood.

Write the phrase *Chip off the Old Block* on the piece of wood near the picture.

Activity Center **Candy Jar**

Fill a baby food jar with colorful candy.

Put the lid on the jar.

Glue pieces of the candy to the jar lid.

Send home as a gift.

Standard Learning Centers

In order to make classrooms appropriate for use with young children, centers where children do the work and exploration are a necessity. Remembering that play is a primary vehicle for and an indicator of their mental growth (NAEYC 1987), most of these centers invite children to "play" with things that are age appropriate, individual appropriate and group appropriate. The materials allow for children to learn, explore, interact physically, emotionally, socially and cognitively (NAEYC 1987).

Purpose of Standard Learning Centers

Standard learning centers are areas designed to **entice** children and to **motivate** them through interaction with a **variety** of **developmentally appropriate materials and equipment**. Children may **choose** activities which are of interest to them, and thus they become **active and interactive learners** (Carroll, 1982, *Learning Centers for Little Kids*).

These centers should not be activity centers where children go to do an assigned activity the way the teacher has designed it. They should **not be work centers where children go to do their ditto sheets** the teacher has assigned. These centers **should not be instruction centers where children go to work in small groups with an adult** whose responsibility it is to instruct them. These centers are **not to be impossible centers where children go to work puzzles or do other activities quietly.**

Physical Arrangement

These centers do require guidelines, limits or rules, whichever you choose to call them. The physical arrangement of the centers should indicate to those in the room (children, staff, parents and visitors) what the physical limits are for each center. Shelves can divide areas from one another.

A table can function as an area.

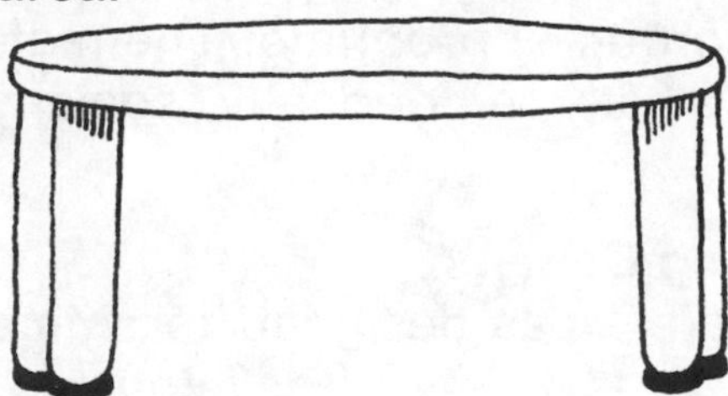

A small piece of carpeting can show the limits for centers.

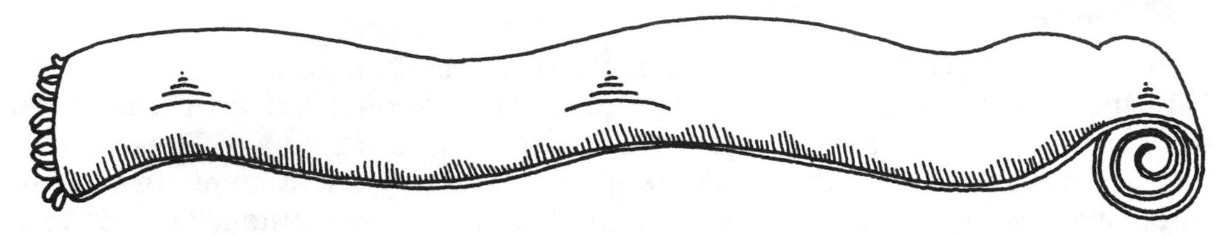

Taped areas on the floor can be used. A large box can house a listening center.

Limits on Materials

There should be limits set on the use of material. When you set these limits, remember to allow for creativity. A block can be used in the blocks, but it might make a wonderful pork chop in the dramatic play center. Pencils are great for the writing center, but they might be needed in the game area to keep score. Children need to be instructed in the appropriate care of the materials, in the use of the materials, in how to make choices about what materials to use, in how to take the materials from the housed places, play with them, clean them up and return them to the appropriate places.

Social Limits

Socially there will need to be boundaries. Children need to talk with the children in their area, but they do not need to shout across the room. They need to be allowed to play alone. They are just learning how to share materials, take turns, cooperate and use manners in their interactions. Take this into consideration and do not require them to share, take turns, cooperate or use manners until they have learned how to do this.

The number of children in the center can aid in group management, social interaction and the controlling of the noise level in the room. Centers should allow for individuals or small groups to interact with each other or provide for the aloneness needed periodically. The number per center can be determined by the physical limits of the center, the quantity of materials and activities in the center, and the social interaction desired in the classroom.

Movement from Center to Center

Movement from center to center should be determined by the children as they are ready to complete one activity or leave it incomplete and move to another area. Children should be able to enter an area where the number of children is less than the number that is allowed in a center. The number allowed in the center should be written at each center in terms that the children can understand—a hand showing the number of children allowed, a set of people cutouts equal to the number allowed, pockets for the children's name cards equal to the number allowed.

Equipment, Physical Placement and Materials
The centers presented in this book are presented by name, equipment needed, proper physical placement and materials that should be in the centers. These materials should be out for children to use, learn with, explore and interact with in their exploration for knowledge.

Choose at least four of these centers to set up permanently in your classroom around the edges of the room. If you find that children are not using the center, leave it alone for a week and they will probably return. If they don't, brainstorm with the children about some new items they might like to see in the center.

Let's Begin
As you begin the year, start with four centers around the edge of the room.

—Present one set of materials per center per day for at least ten days.

—Show the children during large group time how to use each set of materials appropriately.

—Show the children a variety of appropriate things they can do with each set of materials.

—Ask the children if they can think of other appropriate things to do with the materials.

—Place each set of materials where you expect the children to return them when they are finished.

—Assign children to groups of two to four and rotate them through each center for three to five minutes, extending the time when a number of different activities are available in each center.

—Begin using the name cards and pockets to check in and out of the centers even though you are signalling the change and placement yourself.

—Observe the children, the materials, the process carefully this entire time, making sure all rules, procedures and processes are followed.

The Process for the Children

—getting their name cards

—checking into the center

—playing

—cleaning up

—moving to another center

Teacher Instructions: Children in the illustration are left without shading to insure better copying. Color the children's faces the colors to match the races of children in your classroom. Color the picture. Cut out the sign. Mount it on colored poster board. Place in the center.

Art Center

Center Equipment
an easel
child-sized table
child-sized chairs
storage shelves
storage boxes

Center Placement
near a water source
in between active and quiet centers
on uncarpeted surface

Center Materials
plastic knives
paper
masking tape
glue
jars
watercolors
markers
baby oil
tape
crayons (skinny and fat, peeled and unpeeled)
finger paint
sponges
bowls
stapler
sand
clothespins
paintbrushes
scissors
yarn
cookie cutters
pens
dough
ribbon
chalk
saltshakers
pencils
paste
string
glue sticks
paint
tempera
newspaper
smocks
clothesline
rags

Materials for Special Days
sequins
confetti
glitter
puff paint
acrylic paint

Objectives Met at the Art Center

When children are in the art center, they are not only meeting creative, fine motor and art objectives, they might also be seen carrying on these tasks, meeting other objectives:

Math:	counting dabs examining shapes painting numbers
Science:	mixing colors comparing sizes feeling textures
Self-Concept:	I did it myself! exploring without stress
Language Arts:	labeling the pictures chatting while working drawing new things discovered during other times making creations and talking about what these creations can do
Health:	learning to keep the glue out of the mouths washing hands
Safety:	keeping the tools properly stored using utensils appropriately
Music:	singing as they paint adding music to the center
Gross Motor:	An easel with large strokes helps develop arm muscles.
Spatial:	problem solving selection of right size and shape

Teacher Instructions: Children in the illustration are left without shading to insure better copying. Color the children's faces the colors to match the races of children in your classroom. Color the picture. Cut out the sign. Mount it on colored poster board. Place in the center.

Block Center

Center Equipment
storage shelves
storage boxes
dishpan tubs
block bin
block cart

Center Placement
carpeted area
(best to use indoor-outdoor carpet)
place—in a noisy area of the classroom,
—out of pathway,
—near dramatic play,
—where it can be supervised

Center Materials
unit blocks, cubes
large hollow blocks
cardboard bricks
Bristle Blocks
Parquetry Blocks
Duplos, Legos
International Sign Set
large wooden trucks or small wooden trucks
Wooden Storybook City
Jumbo Cubes/Tubes
Lincoln Logs

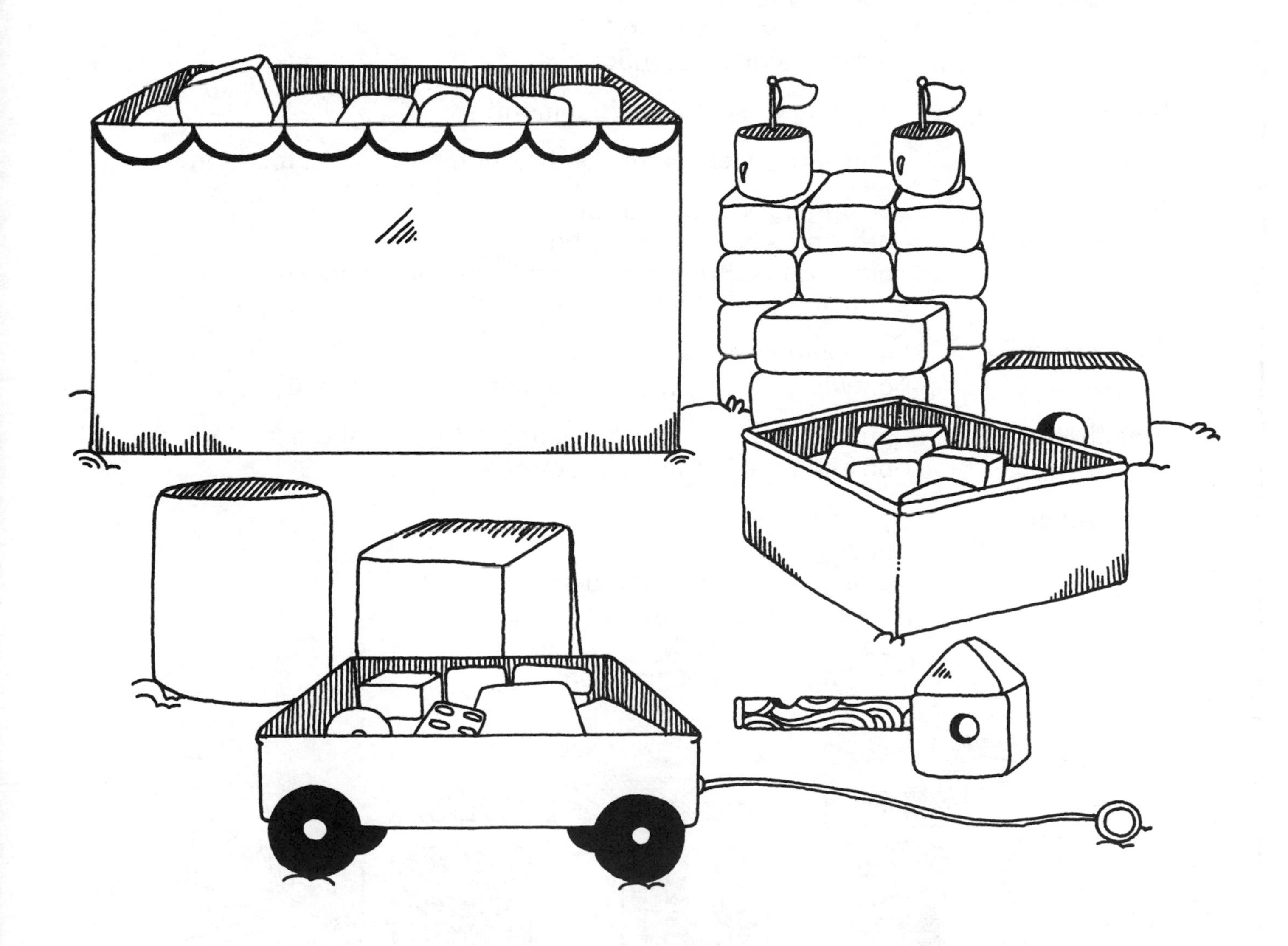

Objectives Met at the Block Center

When children are in the block center, they are not only creating buildings, using their fine and gross motor skills, but they are also meeting these objectives:

Math:	counting the blocks they use examining and getting to know the shapes learning about the sizes of structures putting blocks in order by size measuring the height of the building
Science:	learning how to stack examining textures of the blocks learning about catapulting learning about rolling and other basic physics principles
Social:	learning how to get along next to or with others trading compromising
Language Arts:	chatting while working using new vocabulary making signs for "roads"
Health:	keeping the blocks out of mouths
Safety:	following rules about not throwing or building too high
Art:	designing a "new" structure drawing what they have built making blueprints (white chalk and blue paper) drawing what they would like to build
Gross Motor:	jumping over their structures crawling as they move cars along the built roads
Fine Motor:	putting together the small blocks that are there balancing tall, skinny structures
Self-Concept:	I can do it! having fun doing what they want to do making choices and decisions completing a task feeling of accomplishment

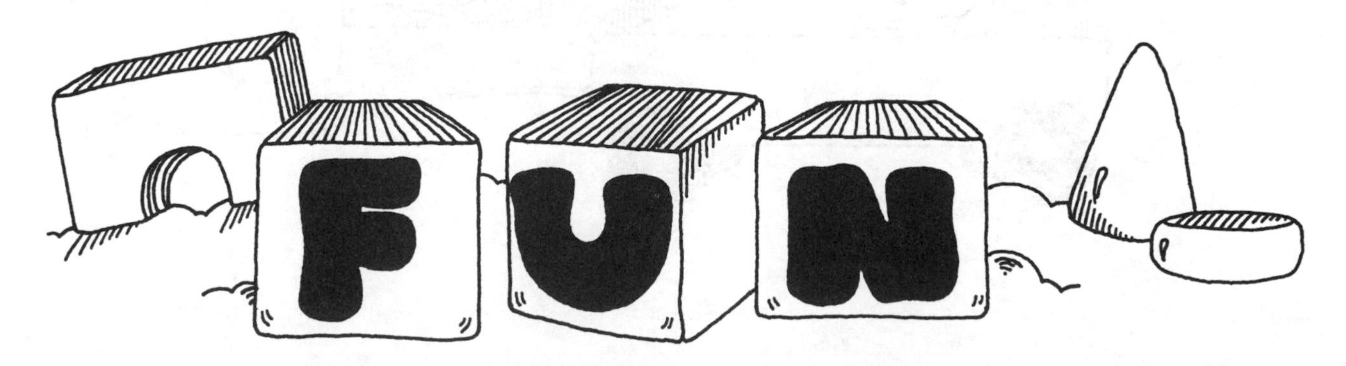

Teacher Instructions: Children in the illustration are left without shading to insure better copying. Color the children's faces the colors to match the races of children in your classroom. Color the picture. Cut out the sign. Mount it on colored poster board. Place in the center.

Dramatic Play Center

Center Equipment
play sink
play stove
play refrigerator
play cupboard
play workbench
child-sized table
child-sized chairs
doll bed
mirror
ironing board/iron

Center Placement
near blocks
in noisy area of room
for easy supervision

Center Materials
plastic flowers
dishes
silverware
doll clothes
hats
purses
backpacks
pots and pans
tools
vases
baby bottle
boots
grocery cart
mop
spray bottle
telephones
jackets
vests
baby blanket
dish drainer
tablecloth
clothes
gloves
lunch boxes
briefcases
tool chest
play food
shoes
strollers
broom
dustpan
typewriter
cradles
ties

Objectives Met at the Dramatic Play Center

When children are in the dramatic play center, they are not only playing out the roles of their families and learning how it feels to be someone, but they are also meeting these objectives:

Math:	setting the table counting out the money for groceries or allowances writing numbers on a grocery list watching the clock
Science:	making concoctions pushing/pulling buggies and strollers using a spray bottle examining water as they wash/dry dishes, babies or clothes
Social:	learning how to get along with others using telephone manners playing the roles of family members
Language Arts:	talking constantly making lists using a computer or typewriter listening to a bedtime story
Health:	"eating" foods washing things to get them clean
Art:	using interior decoration as children decorate their homes
Gross Motor:	pushing strollers hammering
Fine Motor:	setting table changing baby's clothes putting on the clothes in the center eating peas
Self-Concept:	I can do it! having fun doing what they want to do making choices and decisions completing a task feeling of accomplishment
Self-Help:	learning to dress themselves learning to set a table washing their own things

Teacher Instructions: Children in the illustration are left without shading to insure better copying. Color the children's faces the colors to match the races of children in your classroom. Color the picture. Cut out the sign. Mount it on colored poster board. Place in the center.

Gross Motor Center

Center Equipment
storage box
indoor climber
rimball (indoor basketball hoop)
indoor climber

Center Placement
in between noisy and quiet areas
carpeted or uncarpeted area (preferably carpeted)

Center Materials

Velcro balls	balance beam
balls	ropes
scooters	wagons
stompers	roller skates
beanbags	foam targets
ring toss	hula hoops
balance disc	bowling set
pencils	paper
baskets	tape
crayons/markers	

Objectives Met at the Gross Motor Center
When children are in the gross motor center, they are not only developing their large motor skills, but they are also meeting these objectives:

Math:
keeping score in games
measuring the distance to the target
setting up bowling pins in a shape

Social:
working in teams
sharing
compromising
encouraging

Health:
understanding physical well being
learning about their bodies

Creativity:
finding new ways to use scooters

Fine Motor:
picking rings off ring toss
holding many things at once

Self-Concept:
I can do it!
having fun
doing what they want to do
making choices and decisions
completing a task
feeling of accomplishment

Science:
determining speed
calculating distance
examining trajectory
learning about rolling

Language Arts:
chatting
labelling
cheering

Safety:
learning safe motions
looking out for others

Teacher Instructions: Children in the illustration are left without shading to insure better copying. Color the children's faces the colors to match the races of children in your classroom. Color the picture. Cut out the sign. Mount it on colored poster board. Place in the center.

Library Center

Center Equipment
storage shelves
pillows
table/chairs
soft chairs
rocking chair

Center Placement
in a quiet area of
room
an out-of-the way
place

Center Materials
library books
reference books
picture dictionaries
picture books
alphabet books
record player
records/books
tape player
tapes/books
class books made by
the children
word cards
signs
magazines

Objectives Met at the Library Center

When children are in the library center, the main objective is developing pleasure in books, encouraging reading for enjoyment and finding information. In order to meet objectives in a variety of areas, be sure to place books of all kinds in the center—picture books, information books, teachers' books, good literature, classics, new books, legends, fairy tales, nursery rhymes. Be sure to put books covering all areas.

Math:	Books about numbers, shapes, sizes, counting, forming strategies
Science:	Books about animals, weather, people, plants, seeds, tools, etc.
Self-Concept:	Books about the body, children, feeling
Social:	Books about children, getting along, manners, parties, celebrations
Health:	Books about foods, doctors, nurses, dentists, teeth, bodies
Safety:	Books about stop/go, hurting, personal safety
Art:	Caldecott winners, colorful books, how-to-draw books
Music:	Tapes which have excellent musical background music, stories to music *(Peter and the Wolf)*

Teacher Instructions: Children in the illustration are left without shading to insure better copying. Color the children's faces the colors to match the races of children in your classroom. Color the picture. Cut out the sign. Mount it on colored poster board. Place in the center.

Manipulative Center

Center Equipment
shelves
child-sized tables
child-sized chairs
rug squares

Center Placement
a quiet place

Center Materials

buttoning boards
beads
clay
pegs
paper
Ping-Pong balls
pom-poms
tape
foods
potatoes/peeler
flannel board
magnetic board/letters
flannel board story sets
shoestrings
stencils
scissors
muffin tin
small blocks
tweezers
board puzzles
carrots/peeler
apples/peeler
Dressy Bessy
peanuts in the shell
shapes/forms
Play-Doh
Legos
tongs
pencils
paper punch
jigsaw puzzles
Etch a Sketch
hammer/nail sets
Dapper Dan
magnet set
zipping boards
pegboards
Duplos
clothespins
markers
stapler
magic slates
lacing boards
Rig a Jig
tying boards
shape sorters

Objectives Met at the Manipulative Center

Obviously fine motor skills are the basic objective of this center, but many other things happen here, too.

Math:	Children count, make patterns, examine shapes, fit things in holes.
Science:	Children examine textures, squeeze things, use magnets and wonder where all the stuff goes in the Etch-a-Sketch.
Social Studies:	Children work together and learn to do things for themselves or together.
Language Arts:	Children talk, chat and do what they are talking about. They use the magnetic letters to make words. They tell stories with the flannel board.
Safety:	They learn about hammers/nails and workshop safety.
Creativity:	Once they have learned how to do the puzzles, they do them creatively—upside down, without the board, with their eyes shut.
Self-Help:	They learn to eat, lace, tie, peel and do many things alone.

Teacher Instructions: Children in the illustration are left without shading to insure better copying. Color the children's faces the colors to match the races of children in your classroom. Color the picture. Cut out the sign. Mount it on colored poster board. Place in the center.

Game Center

Center Equipment
shelves
carpet squares
small tables
chairs

Center Placement
a slightly noisy place

Center Materials

Games:
- Trivial Pursuit for Juniors
- Clue
- CandyLand
- Monopoly
- Chutes and Ladders
- Junior Pictionary
- Parcheesi
- checkers
- Chinese Checkers
- marbles
- Sorry
- Hi Ho Cherry O
- Boggle
- Twixt
- OhWahRe
- Rook
- Go Fish
- Old Maid
- Rummy
- Easy Money
- dominoes
- UNO
- backgammon
- chess for juniors
- Upwords
- Tiddly-Winks

Objectives Met at the Game Center

Math: Children count the number of spaces they take and check up on others. They learn strategies for problem solving.

Science: Children can learn physics principles of rolling, spinning, trajectory.

Social Studies: Children work together, socialize, learn about winning and losing. Some answers can be learned in Trivial Pursuit.

Language Arts: Children talk and chat about the game and the strategies that they are using.

Motor Skills: Children practice fine motor skills in a meaningful situation.

Teacher Instructions: Children in the illustration are left without shading to insure better copying. Color the children's faces the colors to match the races of children in your classroom. Color the picture. Cut out the sign. Mount it on colored poster board. Place in the center.

Communication Center

Center Equipment
shelves
small tables
chairs

Center Placement
a quiet place

Center Materials

Games:
- alphabet charts
- dictionaries
- Pictionaries
- stationery
- envelopes
- story paper
- lined paper of all sizes and shapes
- unlined paper of all sizes and shapes
- note pads
- notebooks
- journals
- Post-its
- 3" x 5" cards
- 5" x 8" cards
- construction paper
- scissors
- glue
- pencils
- markers
- erasers
- Liquid Paper

Objectives Met at the Communication Center

Math:	Children make lists of things that they need, using numbers.
Social Studies:	Children write letters or notes to others and receive responses. They can get pen pals from other parts of the country and learn about where they live.
Language Arts:	Children talk as they write. They write meaningful messages to others and get responses. They practice word building skills, sentence formation and punctuation.
Motor Skills:	Children practice fine motor skills with meaningful print.
Art:	Children can illustrate their writings.

Teacher Instructions: Children in the illustration are left without shading to insure better copying. Color the children's faces the colors to match the races of children in your classroom. Color the picture. Cut out the sign. Mount it on colored poster board. Place in the center.

Let's Find Out Center

Center Equipment
shelves
small tables
chairs

Center Placement
a quiet place

Center Materials
dictionaries
Pictionaries
note pads
pencils
markers
erasers
Liquid Paper
reference books
- encyclopedias
- science books
- social studies books

open-ended work sheets (See next page.)

Objectives Met at the Let's Find Out Center

Math: Children find things in books, list the page numbers, see sequence.

Social Studies: Children learn that they find out information about different places, people and things in books.

Language Arts: Children read about and record information that they have found in books.

Motor Skills: Children practice fine motor skills with meaningful print.

Art: Children can illustrate their findings as well as write about them.

Students can use the blank ditto sheets that are found in the next few pages at the Let's Find Out Center for any number of investigations.

Let's find out about ____________________.

Find the ____________________ in a book.

What page did you find it on? __________

Copy the picture that you see.

All About ...

Write one thing that appears on the page.

Name ______________________________

Let's find out about ______________________.

Look on page ______________ of the book.

Draw a picture of what you see.

Write about what you see.

Name ____

Scheduling the Centers
Schedules and Contracts

When you set up centers in your classroom, it is always a chore to decide who goes where, when and for how long. This is something you will have to work out, but once you do, some ways are suggested here to help the children know/remember where to go, when and for how long.

Schedule Grids
If you are going to set up your entire classroom in centers and function most of the day that way, the schedule on pages 135 and 136 is suggested. You can ability group your children for reading, math, play, standard centers or activity centers. Place the child's name down the left side, the times and names of centers/activities across the top. Even the youngest children will check their placement after shown only a few times.

Schedule Strips
If children are to go to activity centers in small groups and stay for a short time, label the centers with numbers or colors. Provide them with several 1″ (2.54 cm) squares the colors of the centers. Have them glue the colors on the card in the order that you want them to go to the centers. When they have finished in the center, they put an *X* through that number or color.

Standard Center Selection
Standard centers should be used on a first-come, first-served basis. Children should have a choice of where to go and how long to stay. They can go when they finish their seatwork or activity center work.

However, if you feel that you need to place them in the centers and require them to stay there, pages 137 and 138 give you small pictures of the Standard Center signs. Copy the page so that each child has one of each center. Let the children color the pictures, cut them out and give them to you in an envelope to laminate. Give each laminated set to the children. When you assign centers, have them tape their center cards to a laminated strip of paper 4″ x 16″ (10.16 x 40.64 cm).

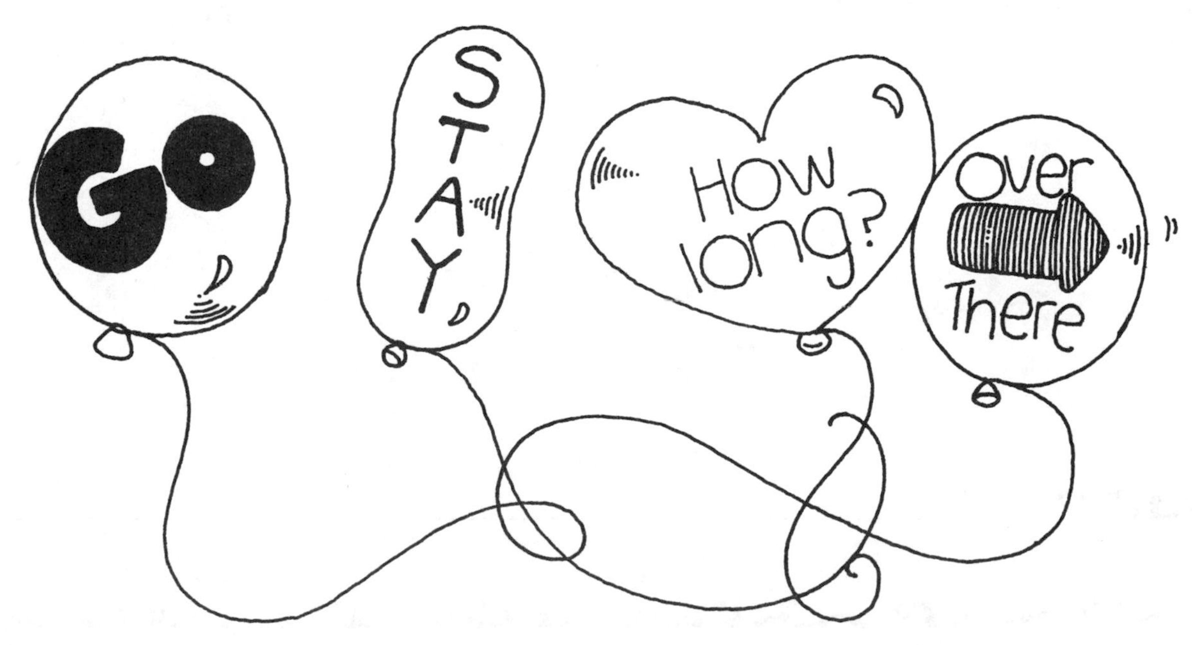

Name	8:30	9:00	9:30	10:00	10:30	11:00	11:30	12:30	1:00	1:30	2:00	2:30
Alice Smith	Math	LA			Recess							
Alan Jones		LA	Math		Recess							
Barbara Holmes		Math	LA		Recess							
Benny Wolfe			LA	Math	Recess							
Carmen Balling	Math			LA	Recess							
Charles Sarber	LA				Recess							
Donald James				LA	Recess							
Elaine Friske	LA				Recess							
Helen Carroll	Math				Recess							
Jeri Glenn			LA		Recess							
Kathy Harper				LA	Recess							
Lorraine Hayes				LA	Recess							
	Math	LA			Recess							

Place child's name in the left-hand column.
Place the subject or center under the proper time slot.

GA1334

Name	8:30	9:00	9:30	10:00	10:30	11:00	11:30	12:30	1:00	1:30	2:00	2:30

Place child's name in the left-hand column.
Place the subject or center under the proper time slot.

Use the pictures that are on these next two pages on contracts for young children to tell them what centers they are to go to during any one period of time. See page 134 for instructions.

NEWS
Library Center
BOOK BAG
comics

Manipulative Center

Communication Center

Game Center
7

Notes
Let's Find Out Center

Monday	Art	Blocks	Red	Yellow	
Tuesday	Green	Red	Blue	Games	
Wednesday	Red	Art	Blocks	Find out	Yellow
Thursday	Blue	Library	Blocks	Green	Play
Friday	Red	Manipul-ative	Yellow	Art	Commu-nication

Weekly Contract

Name ______________________

Week of ______________________

Monday

Tuesday

Wednesday

Thursday

Friday

Have a super week!